THE MAC + CHEESE COOKBOOK

50 Simple Recipes from HOMEROOM,
America's Favorite Mac and Cheese Restaurant

THE MAC + CHEESE COOKBOOK

Allison Arevalo and Erin Wade

Photography by Sara Remington

TEN SPEED PRESS
Berkeley

CONTENTS

RECIPES YOU GREW UP WITH— ONLY BETTER

RECIPES FROM AROUND THE WORLD

CHEMISTRY 59

EXPERIMENTS WITH
UNUSUAL INGREDIENTS

SIDE
DISHES

Extra Credit 75

FINALS 91

DESSERTS

About the Authors 112

Measurement Conversion Charts 113

Index 114

ACKNOWLEDGMENTS

We would both like to thank Homeroom's amazing staff, customers, and the Oakland community for turning our little restaurant dream into a wonderful reality. There isn't a day we don't wake up and feel lucky to get to do something we love and to share it with so many incredible people.

From Allison:

ALEJANDRO—A few short years ago we took a chance, quit our jobs, and moved all the way across the country with hopes of one day opening a restaurant we could call our own. None of this would be possible without you. You listen to my crazy ideas, you put up with—and encourage—my impulsiveness. And you didn't blink an eye when I wanted to sink our life savings into mac and cheese. You have more faith in me than I have in myself, and I feel it every single day. You are my favorite person, my heart and soul, and I love you more than anything.

NICO—My beautiful baby boy, since you arrived, my world got bigger, better, and more beautiful. Your smile and laugh lift my spirits every single day. I cannot wait to share everything this world has to offer with you.

MOM AND DAD—Thank you for teaching me the importance of family, and of sharing life through food and laughter. It's because of you that I chose this path in life, and it's because of you that all my dreams came true. To LENORE, my big sister—your generosity and your big heart guide me through everyday decisions. To GRANDMA—I love sharing my food stories and recipes with you, and carrying on your tradition of providing good food to those you love. And to AUNT LORRAINE— you're my biggest fan, and I never told you how much that means to me.

But it all started with GREAT-GRANDMA FABRIZIO. With fried meatballs, spaghetti with butter sauce, pig skin, and hot peppers from the garden. I miss you every day. You would be so proud to see me now.

CLAUDIA HANSON and SUZANNA LIEM—Thank you for your love, advice, guidance, and for always being there when I need you. You two are the best friends I could have ever hoped for. HERNANDO and CRISTINA—Thank you for all of your blessings and support.

ERIN—Who would have thought that fateful day at Bittersweet Café would have led to this. I am so lucky to have a smart, honest, and extremely capable business partner. But I am even luckier to have an incredible friend. Thank you for making all of this possible. And to your parents, HELEN and AL, you believed in us and gave us the head start we needed. I will always be so grateful.

From Erin:

I would like to thank my family first and foremost for all their *meshugas* and support. ABA—for inspiring me with your homemade mac and cheese, for teaching me how to bake, and for having enough faith in me to give Homeroom the loan that allowed us to open our doors. We could not have done this without you. MOM—an inspirational businesswoman, who introduced me to new flavors and travels that helped shape my tastes and made me successful in the food business. ALEXIS—an amazing sister and my best friend—who listens to me when I'm at my most crazy. STEVO—the person I can share my food obsessions with at the most insane level, and for always being there with a bear hug at the end of a long day. The entire Skowronski clan (JACK, CAROLE, RAFI, DAPHNA, TAMAR, ERIC, SASHA, MEIRAV, and LICHTENSTEINS)—for all of your love and enthusiasm throughout this project, and in whatever we do—one of the best things to happen to me was becoming a part of your family.

To URI—for being an amazing husband, a true friend, and for being willing to take the biggest chance of our lives on my crazy idea to stop being a lawyer and open a mac and cheese restaurant. I absolutely could not have done any of this without your love and support. I love you.

A massive thank-you to all my extended family for their absolute and unwavering awesomeness throughout this project, and the years of building Homeroom that preceded it. I am talking about you BONE BURKE, LINDSEY MANTOAN, KATE REDMAN, THE ROOMIES, NINA AND MORGAN SIMON, MY NOHO CREW, and DIANA ROTHBERG.

To ALLISON—for taking this leap with me and being someone I still love hanging out with after spending more time with you than anyone over the past few years—thanks for being my other Homeroom half.

To my daughter ELLIE—even in my belly you would get excited about good food, jumping around and doing a little jig every time I ate something tasty. I can't wait to share all the recipes in this book with you, as well as all the other fun adventures life has to offer. I love you, little girl.

INTRODUCTION

Hi! We are Erin and Allison—and together we own a restaurant in Oakland, California, dedicated to the best food on earth: macaroni and cheese. A few months ago a neighbor came into our restaurant, Homeroom, to tell us a story about her daughter's first words. The mother explained, "She just kept saying 'ah-ah-chee.' We couldn't figure out what she was referring to until we passed your restaurant and she started yelling 'ah-ah-chee' over and over and then it hit us—'mac and cheese'!"

Whether a child's first words or an adult's cherished food memories, one of the most rewarding parts of owning a mac and cheese restaurant is how people of all ages and backgrounds have deep connections to our food. A close second is turning those connections upside down by making mac and cheese that is even more delectable, rich, and unique than people's best memories.

People ask us all the time for our recipes or for advice on how to improve their own homemade mac and cheese. This book represents everything we've learned after making thousands of mac and cheeses, from recipes to problem-solving. We're excited to bring these ideas beyond the confines of our cheesy little corner of the world and into your home.

About Homeroom

Let's back up a bit to how we got started. You may say it's a modern-day entrepreneurial love story. The two of us met by chance, while sharing a table with our husbands at a crowded café on a rainy Sunday morning. We began chatting about food, traveling, and our general love of cooking and eating. Six months later, we sat in the same café and decided to leave our cushy jobs as a lawyer and marketer respectively, and pour our life savings into a restaurant.

The industry wasn't completely foreign to us. Before becoming a lawyer, Erin worked as both a pastry and line cook at some of the best restaurants in New York City. Meanwhile, Allison learned the craft of customer service by serving at other top restaurants in New York before going into marketing. However, these past restaurant experiences only provided a small taste of what was in store for us when trying to open and run our own place. What followed was a year of blood, sweat, and tears, trying to finance a dream restaurant on a tiny budget and very little experience. Lucky for us, our gamble paid off and Homeroom opened in February 2011. Our restaurant has been packed every day since.

If you're wondering "why mac and cheese?" you're not alone. Almost everyone we meet wonders the same thing. Our answer is pretty simple: it's a dish we love. We grew up on it, and every time we eat a big bowl of creamy mac and cheese, it makes us smile. We thought there were lots of people out there who felt the same way—and luckily, we were right.

At Homeroom, we feature ten different mac and cheeses at a time, and rotate the menu seasonally. We make each dish to order, and they can all be customized with special add-ins like broccoli, bacon, mushrooms, and other tasty ingredients. They are all also available either baked with a topping of toasted panko (Japanese bread crumbs) or served creamy-style (people have deeply held beliefs on which way is better, so we offer both styles for each dish).

When we decided to open Homeroom, there were certain elements of what restaurants call "fine dining" that we wanted to make approachable and available to everyone. We thought it would be fun to have beer/wine and mac pairings on the menu, change the menu seasonally to feature great local produce, and take the time to create homemade traditional American desserts. We also took great pains to make the restaurant space warm, quirky, and inviting with nostalgic school elements—because eating inexpensive food (our entire menu is under ten dollars) should not mean having to sit in cheap chairs under fluorescent lighting.

Our husbands built the tables out of high school bleacher seats, and if you look carefully you'll see sentiments like "Josh loves Stephanie," and "Rachel + Anna were here" carved into the wood. We also installed a vintage library card catalog holder for customers to store their loyalty cards, where each mac and cheese they order earns them a gold star. The entire back wall of the restaurant is a huge chalkboard map of California riddled with doodles reflecting the ethos of each area of the state (yogis and biking hipsters near San Francisco, Hollywood bling in LA).

Although the school theme is sprinkled throughout the restaurant, we also love that the name Homeroom can have another meaning: a room in one's home. We wanted our restaurant to be a place where you feel comfortable and relaxed—as if you were sitting in your own living room. We like to think we achieve this aspect of the name as well, mainly through our incredible staff: the passionate, enthusiastic people who happily greet everyone who walks through the doors.

Most important, we make great mac and cheese, and a lot of it. We serve thousands of mac and cheese dishes every week to people all over the Bay Area as well as visitors from all over the world, which we think makes us the experts in the field. And now we'd like to share what we've learned with you.

BASICS

This cookbook and its recipes are meant to be instructional and easy-to-use, with ingredients you can find whether you live in Oakland or Oklahoma. While there are a lot of fancy, complicated mac and cheese recipes out there, we believe that simpler is better—and that nothing should be expensive, difficult, or intimidating about mac and cheese.

Getting Your Mac On: A Primer on Mac + Cheese

There are a million different ways to make mac and cheese—but we think having one way is a whole lot easier. At Homeroom, we use a base recipe that is the foundation for all of our mac and cheeses. Once you learn it, you can make every recipe in this book as well as any variation you can dream up at home. Since this is Homeroom after all, we've put it into a simple equation:

Pasta + Mac Sauce + Cheese = Mac and Cheese

Basically, every recipe in this book is pasta cooked with cream sauce and cheese—it's a basic formula that can make hundreds of different variations of mac and cheese. We'll teach you each component—how to cook pasta so it's perfect and not mushy and overdone (see page 19). How to make béchamel sauce (we call it Mac Sauce)—the cream sauce that is the foundation for the entire dish (page 9). We'll also teach you how to choose the perfect cheeses to maximize cheesiness, how to bake a mac if you like a crunchy topping, and how to customize each dish to your heart's desire (see pages 7, 14, and 17).

Because each recipe relies on the same formula, we have chosen not to repeat the béchamel/Mac Sauce steps at the beginning of every mac recipe. Each mac starts the same way—by cooking pasta and making Mac Sauce—so you'll want to read this chapter first, and refer back here to the master recipe for making béchamel. Then, each mac recipe focuses on what you add to that base to create a unique and mouthwatering dish.

Turning Mac into a Meal

Although we believe that mac and cheese is a delicious meal all on its own, it's even better when turned into a feast. This is why we've included recipes for complementary veggie-based side dishes as well as desserts. And like all our mac recipes, our goal was to include only recipes that are easy, inexpensive, and approachable to even the most novice of cooks. Lastly, we have included recommendations (see page 20) for beer and wine pairings (we do this at the restaurant, too) if you want to turn your mac meal into a special evening.

The Great Debate: Creamy Versus Baked

At Homeroom we offer our mac and cheeses creamy or baked, because people have *very* strong opinions on how they prefer it. Some folks like gooey, creamy, stovetop-style mac while others crave a crispy baked layer. We designed all the recipes in the cookbook so you can prepare them either way. For some recipes, if we thought they would be best baked, then we included the ingredients and instructions on how to bake it within the recipe. (See page 17 for more information about panko, the Japanese bread crumbs we use in our baked macs.) However, any of the macs in this cookbook can be baked—all you have to do is follow these easy steps.

BASIC BAKED MAC AND CHEESE
WITH CRISPY BREAD CRUMBS

1/2 cup panko (Japanese bread crumbs)

1 prepared mac recipe

LESSON PLAN

1. Preheat the oven to 400°F.

2. Place the bread crumbs on a baking sheet and put it in the oven for about 5 minutes, or until the panko has a lightly brown, toasted color. After you have prepared the mac according to the recipe, place it in an oven-proof dish and sprinkle it with the toasted panko bread crumbs.

3. Bake the mac in the oven until it starts bubbling on the sides, 10 to 15 minutes.

4. Remove from the oven, and eat up!

For the Best-Looking Baked Mac

We've found that the time it takes to bake a mac to get a crunchy top layer and hot interior usually won't turn it brown on its own—just bubbly. To get a beautiful brown topping on any baked mac, we recommend separately toasting the panko beforehand (step 2, above) so you can achieve the same visual effect without overcooking the mac.

MAC SAUCE
(BÉCHAMEL 101)

This simple, creamy, and delicious sauce is the base for all of our mac and cheese recipes. The French call it béchamel. We call it Mac Sauce.

We're pretty certain this sauce will change your life—it has certainly changed ours. Once you learn this recipe, you can make countless varieties of mac and cheese just by adding whatever tasty cheese you like, starting with little else than what you have in your fridge. And the great news is that it's really simple—just flour, butter, milk, and salt. The secret is in the whisk—once you've added the milk, just keep stirring and before you know it, your sauce will be thick, creamy, and the foundation of many awesome mac and cheeses to come.

This recipe makes three cups of sauce—the recipes call for two, but it is wise to make a little extra in case someone wants their mac a bit saucier. It is also somewhat difficult to make only two cups of sauce because you don't have much liquid to work with—so we've found that three is necessary for the easiest preparation. You can use Mac Sauce to make amazing biscuits and gravy if you just fry up bacon and add the bacon grease and chopped up bacon (use our biscuit recipe on page 82 as the base for this). You can also make chicken à la king if you add cooked chicken and peas, and serve it over rice. Mac Sauce is also great as a base or thickener for soups like clam chowder or cream of potato.

A few other things to consider when you are making your Mac Sauce—use whole milk. Don't cut corners and use low-fat or nonfat milk or it will end up tasting watery and gross, resulting in a rather sad-tasting mac and cheese. Also, if you have one around, it's best to use a heavy-bottomed pot to cook the sauce because it will keep the milk from burning and will allow it to cook evenly. One last thing—pay attention to the type of salt you use because it makes a difference (see "A Word on Salt," page 16). **Makes 3 cups**

CONTINUED

3 cups whole milk

1/2 cup unsalted butter

1/2 cup all-purpose flour

2 teaspoons kosher salt or
1 teaspoon table salt

LESSON PLAN

① Heat the milk in a pot over medium heat until it just starts to bubble, but is not boiling, 3 to 4 minutes. Remove from the heat.

② Heat the butter over medium heat in a separate, heavy-bottomed pot. When the butter has just melted, add the flour and whisk constantly until the mixture turns light brown, about 3 minutes. Remove from the heat.

③ Slowly pour the warm milk, about 1 cup at a time, into the butter-flour mixture, whisking constantly. It will get very thick when you first add the milk, and thinner as you slowly pour in the entire 3 cups. This is normal.

④ Once all the milk has been added, set the pot back over medium-high heat, and continue to whisk constantly. In the next 2 to 3 minutes the sauce should come together and become silky and thick. Use the spoon test to make sure it's ready (see picture, opposite). To do this, dip a metal spoon into the sauce—if the sauce coats the spoon and doesn't slide off like milk, you'll know it's ready. You should be able to run your finger along the spoon and have the impression remain. Add the salt.

⑤ The Mac Sauce is ready to use immediately and does not need to cool. Store it in the fridge for a day or two if you want to make it ahead of time—it will get a lot thicker when put in the fridge, so it may need a little milk to thin it out a bit when it comes time to melt in the cheese. Try melting the cheese into the sauce first, and if it is too thick then add milk as needed.

Add the flour to the melted butter, then whisk constantly

Slowly add the warm milk

Keep whisking!!

Don't forget the spoon test

Add the salt

Troubleshooting Mac Sauce

Although Mac Sauce is pretty easy to make, there are a few common mistakes that folks often encounter. The good news is that there are basically only four ways you can screw up, and three of them are easily fixable.

My Mac Sauce came out really runny—it's just like milk.

You probably didn't cook the flour-butter mixture long enough—only when the flour gets nice and toasty before the milk is added does it thicken up the milk properly. The other possibility is that you may not have given the flour and milk enough time to bind together over the heat. If you take your runny sauce and put it back on the stovetop over medium-high heat, and just keep whisking constantly, it will soon thicken up! This takes a little longer—but still should only be about ten minutes before you notice that your sauce is getting thick, rich, and creamy looking.

My Mac Sauce has brown flecks in it.

If you see little brown flecks and taste a nutty flavor, it means you overcooked the butter-flour mixture and the flour was actually toasted instead of just cooked. When the flour is toasted it gets a nutty taste, and it becomes harder to fully incorporate it into the milk. If the taste doesn't bother you, don't worry about it. Next time, add the milk a little sooner.

If it does bother you, unfortunately you've got to start from square one. However, we recommend adding some cheese to a little sample of the sauce. Sometimes, people detect the nuttiness in the sauce alone, but with the cheese added, it's not noticeable.

My Mac Sauce is so thick—it's hard to even melt the cheese into it!

Don't worry—there's still hope! You just cooked the milk and flour mixture together for a little too long so the sauce thickened too much. Simply add milk to thin it out to the desired consistency (we recommend doing this when you add the cheese), and you'll be fine!

My Mac Sauce is not smooth—why does it have clumps in it?

Your problem is that you did not whisk fast enough when you added the milk. Or, if you were using anything other than a whisk, you might also get clumps. When we told you to whisk constantly when you add the milk to the butter-flour mixture—we meant it! You really do have to whisk all the time once the milk is added until the sauce is complete to ensure you end up with a smooth sauce. The good news is that once you add the cheese and noodles to your sauce, you probably won't notice those little clumps. If you want perfection, redo the recipe. But most people will be pretty happy to eat homemade mac and cheese—even with a few clumps in there.

Mac 101: Mac-Making Advice from the Pros

We know what you are thinking. Macaroni and cheese—how hard can this be? Well, it's not hard—but there are a lot of tricks of the trade that will help make it even more delicious. After cooking thousands upon thousands of mac and cheeses for hungry fans, we've learned many little lessons that will help make your mac the yummiest possible. Here, we reveal our secrets for the first time.

Choosing Cheeses

TIP #1. MORE AGE = MORE CHEESY FLAVOR

Just as people get more complex with age, so does cheese. If you want to make a really tasty Cheddar-y mac, you will get a more cheesy taste using an eighteen-month–aged Cheddar (like we do at Homeroom) instead of a six-month–aged Cheddar. A lot of cheap supermarket Cheddars are aged for only three months, and although they may look orange, they won't taste very Cheddar-y. Buy Cheddars that are aged a longer amount of time—a commonly available, exceptional super-market brand is Tillamook Special Reserve (aged fifteen months). Even Tillamook Sharp (aged nine months) will work. Not all cheeses in this cookbook need to be flavorful—anytime you see Jack or Havarti in a recipe, we are using them specifically because they are creamy and not flavorful, and because we want to highlight other flavors in the dish (either another cheese or other ingredients). So don't worry about seeking out aged versions of these cheeses. For cheeses like Cheddar, Parmesan, pecorino, or blue cheese though—you will thank us if you go for the older stuff.

TIP #2. DON'T WASTE YOUR MONEY ON SUPER-FANCY CHEESES

When we started to write this cookbook, we were so excited to play with all sorts of fancy cheeses. We don't use these cheeses at the restaurant because they're generally expensive, and we are committed to keeping our prices below ten dollars. However, we soon found that a lot of cheeses we enjoy eating on a cheese plate make absolutely disgusting mac and cheeses. An example: we love British farmstead Cheddars (like anything made by Neal's Yard Dairy) and wanted to make an English mac with them. However, the rustic flavors that make a farmstead Cheddar delicious on a cheese plate were just plain gross when concentrated in a mac. No matter what we did, it tasted like eating a barnyard. Buttery French cheeses literally tasted like butter when melted into a mac—and not in a good way. The great news is that while we have always been committed to making the best mac and cheeses

Carmody

Parmesan

Cheddar

Pecorino

Point Reyes Blue

White Cheddar

that are approachable and affordable for all, it was liberating to discover that more expensive cheeses do not equal more delicious mac and cheeses. As a result, this cookbook is filled with recipes in which all the ingredients should be available regardless of where you live and what kind of markets you have available.

TIP #3. SALT IS A CHEESE'S BEST FRIEND

If you have added the proper amount of cheese to your mac, but it still doesn't taste "cheesy" enough, chances are the problem is not cheese, but salt. Salt brings out the flavors of all kinds of food—meat, chocolate, bread—but it is particularly noticeable with mac and cheese. So if your mac isn't tasting as cheesy as you want, don't start grating more cheese. Try adding a bit more salt first, and see if you don't notice a huge difference.

A Word on Salt

Many chefs like to have an array of fancy salts on hand for cooking, but at Homeroom, we only use two: kosher salt and table (or iodized) salt. You can cook with either one, but we prefer to use table salt for baking, and kosher salt for cooking. What's the difference? Well, because of the iodine that is added to table salt, it can give food a slightly metallic flavor—although the tiny grains are perfect for baking because they easily disperse throughout dough. Kosher salt has lighter, bigger flakes and no chemical flavor. You don't have to be quite as careful when you add it to food, and we prefer it in all our cooking because of its taste and versatility. Kosher salt has bigger flakes and packs less of a salty punch than table salt.

If you are substituting table salt for kosher salt in recipes that call for the latter in this cookbook, you cannot use the same amount or you will end up with a salty, unpalatable mess. Because the Mac Sauce is so critical to a good mac and cheese, we did the conversion in that recipe for you—but in other recipes, if you are substituting table salt for kosher salt, use less than the recipe calls for. A good general rule of thumb is to use half as much table salt as you would kosher salt.

Customizing Your Mac

TIP #1. PANKO KICKS THE BOOTY OF REGULAR BREAD CRUMBS

If you are making a baked mac, all of our recipes call for Japanese panko bread crumbs. Panko is the crispiest, crunchiest bread crumb you've ever tasted—each one pops with crunch. Regular bread crumbs—whether homemade or store-bought—tend to be a little chewy, which we have found to give an unpleasant texture to mac and cheese. Panko makes a perfect crust every time, and is stocked in the international section of any grocery store. If you want a brown, toasty color to the crust, just toss the panko on a baking sheet at 400°F until it turns the color brown you are looking for, about 5 minutes. Then use it in the recipe as directed. But we didn't add that step in the recipes that use panko, because the flavor is the same, even if you don't toast it on its own first.

TIP #2. DON'T BE AFRAID TO EXPERIMENT

You can customize all of our recipes to include your favorite ingredients. At Homeroom, we have a large list of add-ins that customers can mix with any mac—everything from peas to bacon to caramelized onions. We recommend having your favorite add-in on hand. Pull out a few spoonfuls of the finished mac, and taste it with the add-in you want to put in. You'll know immediately if it's a winner or if it's better off left out.

Tasty Add-In Suggestions

Bacon, chorizo, grilled chicken, hot dog, sausage, ground beef or pork (avoid bigger cuts of meat like chopped steak because the texture will be tougher than the mac and won't blend very well), peas, sautéed mushrooms, spinach, artichoke hearts, caramelized onions, broccoli, roasted butternut squash, asparagus, garlic

Choosing and Cooking Noodles

TIP #1. USE THE RIGHT NOODLE

You can't have a mac and cheese without the "mac," and choosing the right mac is just as important as selecting the right cheese.

We spent months looking for the perfect noodle. We could picture it clear as day: a large curved elbow with deep ridges and thick walls. (At Homeroom, we use the Ronzoni brand, which is widely available. Barilla is another good choice.) It sounds simple, but was surprisingly hard to find. Most noodles we tested were either too small, too thin, or the wrong shape. A noodle with any of these characteristics can ruin a mac and cheese, and here's why:

If your noodles are small, like the baby elbows you often see in boxed mac and cheese, they will fall apart when you cook them. They simply can't withstand being cooked twice: once in boiling water, and again in the cheese sauce. This is also true of thin noodles. If your uncooked noodle falls apart easily when you press it between two fingers, you have a thin noodle, and one that will turn to mush in a mac and cheese.

We wanted the noodles at Homeroom to be shaped like an elbow because that's what we remember eating as kids, but also because the elbow helps capture the cheese sauce. Shapes like penne, orecchiette, and rigatoni work well too, because like elbows, they have hollow centers that fill with cheese when drenched in sauce. Stay away from long noodles, like spaghetti, fettuccine, or linguine. The cheese sauce will slide right off and you'll be left with a pool of cheese sauce and nothing to sop it up with.

This may not seem like it needs explaining, but cooking your noodles properly is essential to a good mac and cheese. First, read the directions on the package. Cooking times will vary depending on the shape and brand of your pasta, so we can't tell you exactly how long they should cook. We can tell you, though, to cook the noodles for slightly less time than the directions say for "al dente." Al dente means "to the tooth" in Italian—noodles that have some bite to them. If you cook your noodles a little less than al dente, they'll be slightly undercooked and won't get mushy when mixed with a hot cheese sauce.

Choose a large pot for your noodles, and fill it three-quarters of the way up with water—the noodles should have plenty of room to swim around in the boiling water. If the pot is too small or if there isn't enough water in the pot, the water will get super starchy and the pasta will get a weird, sticky texture.

When the water comes to a full boil, add a generous sprinkle of salt. This adds a bit of flavor to the noodles. Next, drop the noodles into the pot, and give them a good stir. This helps prevent them from sticking together.

When your noodles are done, quickly drain them and run under cold water to stop the cooking process. If you're using them right away, you're good to go. If not, put them in a bowl and drizzle them with a little neutral-flavored oil (like canola oil) to prevent them from sticking together.

A Note on Portion Size

We've designed our mac recipes to serve up a soul-satisfying portion of rich-and-cheesy goodness to four people. But if your crew is really hungry or you're not planning on side dishes, you may find they better serve three people.

Choosing Beers and Wines to Pair with Macs

Throughout the book, you'll notice that we paired each mac and cheese recipe with a specific wine or beer. We do the same thing at Homeroom, not only because we think beer and wine pair extremely well with our macs, but also because we wanted to make it part of our restaurant's experience.

When we were planning the type of restaurant we wanted to open, it was important to us to provide a fine-dining experience, without the expense or hassle of going to a fancy restaurant. For us, this meant personal service that was friendly and inviting, with high-quality, local ingredients, and a stellar beer and wine selection that we could pair with each dish.

We're not the world's greatest experts, but we do follow a few general rules when we decide on our pairings. Overall, we balance flavors. A good pairing for us means that you can appreciate the nuance of flavors in the drink as well as the dish. Nothing should be overshadowed or overexposed. A spicy mac pairs with a hoppy beer and a bold wine. A subtle cheese pairs with a crisp blonde ale and a delicate pinot. Keep the characteristics of the entire dish in mind—an acidic dish will pair well with an acidic wine, and a sweet beer will taste great with a slightly sweet meal (think malty lager with barbecued ribs). If you keep your flavors balanced, you can perfectly pair any dish with the drink of your choice.

As an example, here are two pairings that we use at Homeroom, and why we think they work so well:

Vermont White Cheddar Mac (page 31) with Old Rasputin Stout: In this pairing, the chocolaty sweetness of the stout brings out the subtle sweetness of the cheese, without it being overpowering. Both the dish and the beer are rich and decadent with a velvety mouthfeel, so neither one gets lost.

Mexican Mac (page 48) with Tempranillo: The fiery chipotles in the Mexican mac perfectly tame the smokiness of the Tempranillo. The wine is also slightly acidic, which pairs nicely with the citrusy lime. Overall, this a pairing of bold with bold, so you still get to appreciate the variety of flavors in both the wine and the mac.

Gluten-Free Mac and Cheese

At the restaurant we provide the option for each one of our macs to be prepared gluten-free. This means instead of using regular semolina pasta, we use quinoa pasta, although you can also use brown rice pasta or any gluten-free pasta you prefer. We also use tapioca flour instead of wheat flour in our Mac Sauce; however, you can substitute almost any gluten-free flour. After testing all possible flours and pastas, we think that quinoa pasta and tapioca flour work the best, but it's a matter of personal preference.

All you have to do is make these two replacements and you can make any mac and cheese recipe in this cookbook gluten-free. Another quick note—you cannot bake a mac with panko if you want it to be gluten-free. However, you can bake the mac with a bit of sprinkled cheese instead, or find a gluten-free bread crumb topping that you prefer. Regardless, we're sure you'll really enjoy it and hope you'll find that mac and cheese is actually one of the most versatile gluten-free dishes you can prepare.

Classic Mac 25

Jalapeño Popper Mac 26

Spicy Mac 27

Trailer Mac 28

Tuna Mac 30

Vermont White Cheddar Mac 31

Chili Mac 32

Smoky Bacon Mac 34

Breakfast Mac 37

Gilroy Garlic Mac 39

American Classics

RECIPES YOU GREW UP WITH—ONLY BETTER

American Classics aren't only books you read—they are things you remember. They're ice cream cones, apple pie, gym class, parades, homeroom, and mac and cheese.

The macs that follow are the staples of our menu, and for good reason. They are reminiscent of the mac and cheese (and other foods) you ate as a child, with a twist or two that makes them more enjoyable than you remember. Things like tuna casserole, hot dogs, jalapeño poppers, and bacon and eggs. The macs that immediately remind you of childhood are so obviously American, you couldn't possibly call them anything else.

We love re-creating childhood favorites not only because they're tasty, but also because they make people smile. Everything at Homeroom, from the library card catalog and the paper airplanes to the Chili Mac and the Tuna Mac, brings back fond memories for everyone who walks through the door.

Maybe that's why they keep coming back for more.

CLASSIC MAC

This is it. The super-creamy, extra-cheesy mac and cheese you grew up with. Wait. We take that back. This is far better than anything that plops out of a foiled "cheese packet" or sprinkles out of a little sealed bag. Out of all our recipes, this one took the longest to create. We tested hundreds of cheese combinations until finally we found something worthy of the dish we wanted to be most proud of at Homeroom. It was a moment of true magic. The winning combination? One-quarter salty pecorino to three-quarters two-year–aged, extra-sharp yellow Cheddar.

Who would have thought it could be that simple? **Serves 4**

1/2 pound dried elbow pasta

2 cups Mac Sauce (page 9)

1 1/2 cups grated 2-year-aged, extra-sharp Cheddar cheese

1/2 cup grated Pecorino Romano cheese

BEER PAIRING: Nutty Brown Ale

WINE PAIRING: Meritage

LESSON PLAN

1. Cook the pasta in salted boiling water until a little less than al dente. Drain, rinse the pasta with cold water, and drain it again.

2. Add the sauce and both cheeses to a large, heavy-bottomed pot and cook over medium heat. Stir until the cheese is barely melted, about 3 minutes. Slowly add the cooked pasta, stir, and continue cooking while stirring continuously until the pasta is hot and steaming, another 5 minutes.

3. Spoon into bowls and enjoy!

    VARIATIONS: Or, get creative. Add things like broccoli, peas, hot peppers, or bacon when you add the cooked pasta. You can also sprinkle a little panko on top and cook in a 400°F oven for 10 to 15 minutes for a version that's crispy on top and creamy inside.

JALAPEÑO POPPER MAC

We created this mac for a Super Bowl party we threw at Homeroom. We wanted to invent a dish to mimic our absolute favorite game-day snack. This mac and cheese is essentially a deconstructed jalapeño popper, where you break through a crispy outer shell to get a bite of gooey, Cheddar-y cream cheese filling studded with jalapeño chiles. It is ridiculously decadent, and if you make it for your next game-day party, you will be sure to be a winner even if your favorite team is not. **Serves 4**

1/2 pound dried elbow pasta

2 cups Mac Sauce (page 9)

2 cups grated sharp Cheddar cheese

1/2 cup cream cheese

1/4 cup stemmed, seeded, and chopped jalapeño chiles, plus extra, for garnish

1/2 cup panko (Japanese bread crumbs)

BEER PAIRING: IPA

WINE PAIRING: Barbera

LESSON PLAN

① Preheat the oven to 400°F.

② Cook the pasta in salted boiling water until a little less than al dente. Drain, rinse the pasta with cold water, and drain it again.

③ Add the sauce, Cheddar, cream cheese, and chiles to a large, heavy-bottomed pot and cook over medium heat. Stir until the cheese is barely melted, about 3 minutes. Turn off the heat and stir in the cooked pasta. Take a taste to check the potency of the chiles—jalapeños can vary in their heat, depending on the batch and season, so you may want to add more to increase the fire.

④ Pour the cheesy noodle mixture into a large baking dish. Top evenly with panko and bake until you see the cheese sauce bubbling up the sides, 10 to 15 minutes.

⑤ Spoon into bowls and serve immediately. Sprinkle a few extra jalapeño bits on top for an extra kick.

SPICY MAC

Although we generally steer clear of obscure ingredients, this particular recipe uses marash pepper flakes, which can be a little challenging to find. This spice comes from Turkey, and if you are about to flip the page because you don't want to buy an ingredient just for one mac recipe—let us convince you otherwise. We add marash pepper to our spicy mac because we've had a longstanding love affair with this particular ingredient. Unlike regular red pepper flakes, marash pepper flakes are slightly smoky, rich in peppery flavor, and have a milder heat. They can be sprinkled on everything from pasta to scrambled eggs to add a delicious kick to pretty much anything you would normally add red pepper flakes or hot sauce to. Start with 2 teaspoons; you can always add more. We order ours online at wholespice.com, but any great spice shop worth its salt (ha!) should carry it.

You can make this recipe without the marash pepper if you can't find it. The dish will still be tasty, but it will lack that special something that makes ours so addictive (and frankly, so spicy...). Also, we recommend adding a bit of extra salt to this recipe since pepper Jack is generally not a very salty cheese and might taste a little flat without extra salt. **Serves 4**

1/2 pound dried elbow pasta

2 cups Mac Sauce (page 9)

2 cups grated pepper Jack cheese

2 teaspoons marash pepper flakes (see headnote)

Kosher salt, to taste

BEER PAIRING: Vienna-style Lager (e.g., Negra Modelo)

WINE PAIRING: Chenin Blanc

LESSON PLAN

1. Cook the pasta in salted boiling water until a little less than al dente. Drain, rinse the pasta with cold water, and drain it again.

2. Add the sauce, the cheese, and the pepper flakes to a large, heavy-bottomed pot and cook over medium heat. Stir until the cheese is barely melted, about 3 minutes. Slowly add the cooked pasta, stir, and continue cooking while stirring continuously until the dish is nice and hot, another 5 minutes.

3. Taste the dish for desired spice—add more marash pepper if you want to up the heat, or more salt if you think it's needed. Spoon into bowls and serve immediately.

TRAILER MAC

The ironic country cousin of our classic mac and cheese, trailer mac is made with creamy Cheddar sauce and chopped hot dog, then topped with crushed potato chips. Trailer Mac is the first mac and cheese we ever served, and it has a permanent place both on our menu and in our hearts. After asking dozens of people what their favorite ways to eat mac and cheese were, we invented Trailer Mac by combining the two most popular responses: with hot dogs and potato chips. At first we thought that these suggestions sounded kind of gross. But when we tried it, we understood how these two elements combine to create the perfect dish. The hot dog flavor permeates the cheese and fills the dish with a rich, meaty flavor, while the chips add great texture to every bite. Try it and you'll understand why it has its own cult following. **Serves 4**

1/2 pound dried elbow pasta

2 cups Mac Sauce (page 9)

2 cups grated sharp Cheddar cheese

1/2 to 1 cup chopped hot dogs

2 cups crushed potato chips, for topping

BEER PAIRING: Pilsner (or PBR, for irony)

WINE PAIRING: Sangiovese

LESSON PLAN

① Cook the pasta in salted boiling water until a little less than al dente. Drain, rinse the pasta with cold water, and drain it again.

② Add the sauce, the Cheddar, and the hot dogs to a large, heavy-bottomed pot and cook over medium heat. Stir until the cheese is barely melted, about 3 minutes. Slowly add the cooked pasta, stir, and continue cooking while stirring continuously until the dish is nice and hot, another 5 minutes.

③ Spoon into bowls, sprinkle with potato chips, and serve immediately.

TUNA MAC

Inspired by the classic American tuna casserole, Tuna Mac is the ultimate comfort food. Serving up hunks of tuna in a rich and creamy Havarti sauce studded with little peas that pop in your mouth—this dish quickly became one of our best sellers. What makes this mac so delicious is that we don't just throw in plain canned tuna. It's built on an incredible stand-alone tuna salad. Like what you'd be happy to have on a sandwich if you have extra. The complex flavors of the tuna salad go a long way to elevate the flavor of the entire dish. It's just like Grandma's tuna casserole, only better. **Serves 4**

1/2 pound dried elbow pasta

TUNA SALAD

16 ounces canned tuna in water, drained

1/4 cup finely chopped onion

2 tablespoons drained capers

1/4 cup mayonnaise

1/2 cup finely chopped celery

2 teaspoons kosher salt

1/4 to 1/2 teaspoon freshly ground black pepper

MAC

2 cups Mac Sauce (page 9)

2 cups grated Havarti cheese

1 cup frozen peas, thawed

1 cup crushed potato chips or crushed oyster crackers, for topping (optional)

BEER PAIRING: Hefeweizen or Blonde

WINE PAIRING: Sauvignon Blanc

LESSON PLAN

1. Cook the pasta in salted boiling water until a little less than al dente. Drain, rinse the pasta with cold water, and drain it again.

2. To make the salad: In a bowl, combine all the ingredients until they are incorporated and evenly distributed. Season with salt and pepper to taste.

3. To make the mac: Add the sauce, Havarti, 1 cup of the tuna salad (save the rest for a sandwich, or whatever else you'd like), and the peas to a large, heavy-bottomed pot and cook over medium heat. Stir until the cheese is barely melted, about 3 minutes. Slowly add the cooked pasta, stir, and continue cooking while stirring continuously until the dish is nice and hot, another 5 minutes.

4. Spoon into bowls, top with crushed potato chips or crushed crackers, and serve.

VERMONT WHITE CHEDDAR MAC

We don't exactly know what it is about those cheesemakers in Vermont, but after test-ing hundreds of white Cheddars from around the country, we can safely say they make the tastiest Cheddar around. As soon as you cut into a chunk of it, you can see the fla-vor crystals screaming out goodness. Pop quiz: Do you know what those little crystals are? They are bunches of amino acids called tyrosine, and if you see them, it means you found a good, aged cheese. Typically cheeses aged for at least two years will have some of these delectable little crystals.

This mac is perfect for trying all sorts of add-ins—everything from chorizo and hot dogs to mushrooms and peas. Get creative and you really can't go wrong. **Serves 4**

1/2 pound dried elbow pasta

2 cups Mac Sauce (page 9)

2 cups grated sharp, aged Vermont white Cheddar cheese

BEER PAIRING: **Stout**

WINE PAIRING: **Shiraz**

LESSON PLAN

1. Cook the pasta in salted boiling water until a little less than al dente. Drain, rinse with cold water, and drain the pasta again.

2. Add the sauce and cheese to a large, heavy-bottomed pot and cook over medium heat. Stir until the cheese is barely melted, about 3 minutes. (At this point, throw in your choice of add-ins.) Slowly add the cooked pasta, stir, and continue cooking while stirring continuously until the dish is nice and hot, another 5 minutes.

3. Spoon into bowls and enjoy!

CHILI MAC

Along with the Jalapeño Popper Mac, we invented this recipe for a Super Bowl party that we threw at the restaurant. We serve chili throughout the winter as its own dish, and can't get enough of the spicy richness topped with a little bit of sour cream and Cheddar. This recipe makes much more chili than needed for the mac—our hope is that you will enjoy the chili on its own one night (it's delicious with shredded Cheddar, cilantro, and a bit of sour cream), and make Chili Mac the next! If you are feeling lazy, you can always just use canned chili, but it will be nowhere near as tasty as whipping up a batch of the fresh stuff. **Serves 4**

CHILI

6 tablespoons olive oil or vegetable oil

1 red bell pepper, cored, seeded, and chopped into 1/2-inch chunks

1 green bell pepper, cored, seeded, and chopped into 1/2-inch chunks

1 jalapeño chile, stemmed, seeded, and finely chopped

1 onion, diced

1 pound ground beef

1 tablespoon kosher salt

1 tablespoon chili powder

1 teaspoon cayenne pepper

1 teaspoon dried oregano

1 tablespoon ground cumin

1 (16-ounce) can black beans, drained

1 (16-ounce) can pinto beans, drained

1 (16-ounce) can crushed tomatoes

LESSON PLAN

1. To make the chili: In a large pot, heat the olive oil over medium-high heat. Add the bell peppers, chile, and onion and sauté until tender, about 10 minutes.

2. Add the ground beef, and stir to break up the beef into small chunks. When the beef begins to brown (after a few minutes), add the salt, chili powder, cayenne pepper, oregano, and cumin. Cook for 2 more minutes to allow the spices to become fragrant.

3. Add the beans and canned tomatoes with juice. Cook until the mixture reaches a boil. Turn off the heat, taste (add more salt if necessary), and use for the Chili Mac or serve on its own.

MAC

1/2 pound dried elbow pasta

2 cups Mac Sauce (page 9)

2 cups grated sharp
Cheddar cheese

BEER PAIRING: Red Ale

**WINE PAIRING: Cabernet
Sauvignon**

④ To make the mac: Cook the pasta in salted boiling water until a little less than al dente. Drain, rinse the pasta with cold water, and drain it again.

⑤ Add the sauce, the Cheddar, and 2 cups of the chili to a large, heavy-bottomed pot and cook over medium heat. Stir until the cheese is barely melted, about 3 minutes. Slowly add the cooked pasta, stir, and continue cooking while stirring continuously until the dish is nice and hot, another 5 minutes.

⑥ If you want more chili flavor, you can always add more chili to taste (the dish, not the powder). Spoon into bowls and serve hot.

SMOKY BACON MAC

It's true that you can add bacon to any of the macs in this book and the result will probably be delicious. But since we designed this mac around the salty, smoky taste of bacon, we think it's the best choice if you're craving a big dose of pork.

The intense flavor of smoky cheese goes a long way. Even the smallest shred of a smoked Cheddar or Jack will impart a whole lot of flavor to your mac and cheese, so go easy on it. This hearty mac makes a great dish for the winter holidays. (Can't you just see it sitting pretty next to a big, plump turkey?) **Serves 4**

1/2 pound dried elbow pasta

1 pound sliced bacon

2 cups Mac Sauce (page 9)

1 cup grated smoked Cheddar cheese

1 cup grated Jack cheese

BEER PAIRING: Red Ale

WINE PAIRING: Cabernet Sauvignon

LESSON PLAN

1. Cook the pasta in salted boiling water until a little less than al dente. Drain, rinse with cold water, and drain the pasta again.

2. Cook the bacon in a frying pan over high heat until crispy, about 8 minutes. Remove extra grease by patting the strips with a paper towel, and then cut into bite-size pieces.

3. Add the sauce and both cheeses to a large, heavy-bottomed pot and cook over medium heat. Stir until the cheese is barely melted, about 3 minutes. Add the bacon and stir to combine. Slowly add the cooked pasta, stir, and continue cooking while stirring continuously until the dish is nice and hot, another 5 minutes.

4. Spoon into bowls and serve hot.

Roasted Carrots with
Citrus Vinaigrette (page 78)

BREAKFAST MAC

Great for breakfast, but this one's also pretty darn amazing any time of the day. When we were testing recipes for a breakfast mac, we kept sensing that something was missing. Then Rafi, Erin's brother-in-law and taste-tester that day, casually asked: "Why don't you throw an egg on top?"

So Rafi, if we haven't told you before, you're a genius! Bake this one in individual bread crumb–topped portions. After baking, slide on a fried egg. When you break into the runny egg, you get egg yolk, bacon, and creamy sharp Cheddar with each spoonful. This mac is completely to blame for the five extra pounds we each gained this year. It's okay. Every single bite was completely worth it. **Serves 4**

1/2 pound dried elbow pasta

1/2 pound sliced bacon

2 cups Mac Sauce (page 9)

2 cups grated extra-sharp, aged Cheddar cheese

1/2 cup panko (Japanese bread crumbs)

2 tablespoons unsalted butter

4 large eggs

Freshly ground black pepper

BEER PAIRING: IPA
WINE PAIRING: Rosé

LESSON PLAN

1. Cook the pasta in salted boiling water until a little less than al dente. Drain, rinse with cold water, and drain the pasta again.

2. Preheat the oven to 400°F.

3. Cook the bacon in a frying pan over high heat until crispy, about 8 minutes. Remove extra grease by patting the strips with a paper towel, and then cut into bite-size pieces.

4. Add the sauce and cheese to a large, heavy-bottomed pot and cook over medium heat. Stir until the cheese is barely melted, about 3 minutes. Add the bacon and stir to combine. Slowly add the cooked pasta, stir, and continue cooking while stirring continuously until the dish is nice and hot, another 5 minutes.

CONTINUED

⑤ Spoon the mac and cheese into 4 individual, 5-inch-diameter ovenproof bowls. Sprinkle the panko evenly on top of each bowl. Bake until bubbly, 10 to 15 minutes.

⑥ While the macs are cooking, fry the eggs: Melt 1 tablespoon of the butter in a large sauté pan over medium-high heat. Crack 2 of the eggs into the pan, cover, and let cook undisturbed for 3 to 4 minutes. The eggs are done when all the egg white is completely opaque, and the yolk is still nice and bright. Slide the eggs onto a plate and repeat with the remaining tablespoon of butter and 2 eggs.

⑦ Remove the macs from the oven, and slide a fried egg on top of each one. Top each egg with some black pepper. Serve immediately.

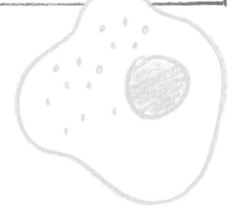

GILROY GARLIC MAC

Ah, the Gilroy. The all-time best-selling mac on the Homeroom menu. Named after the pleasantly stinky, garlic-growing town in central California, the Gilroy Mac is a little garlicky, super-creamy, and utterly addictive. To make the Gilroy especially delicious, we use a compound butter by mixing together minced garlic and room-temperature butter. Compound butters are easy to make, and add a ton of flavor to all sorts of dishes.

We cook massive amounts of mac and cheese at festivals around the Bay Area, and this is usually the mac we make because it best showcases the type of food you'll find at the restaurant. At Outside Lands, a three-day music festival in San Francisco's Golden Gate Park, we dish out thousands of portions of Gilroy Mac. This translates to 1,000 pounds of pasta, 1,200 pounds of cheese, and 125 gallons of Mac Sauce. Our staff works around the clock in our tiny kitchen to make it happen—but when we see hundreds of people waiting in line for a taste of the Gilroy, it makes it all worthwhile.

And we got to see Stevie Wonder live. That was pretty cool, too. **Serves 4**

4 large cloves garlic, minced

3 tablespoons unsalted butter, at room temperature

1/2 pound dried elbow pasta

2 cups Mac Sauce (page 9)

1 1/2 cups grated Gouda cheese

1/2 cup grated Pecorino Romano cheese

BEER PAIRING: Belgian Saison

WINE PAIRING: Chardonnay

LESSON PLAN

① In a small bowl, mash together the minced garlic and the butter to form a compound butter.

② Cook the pasta in salted boiling water until a little less than al dente. Drain, rinse with cold water, and drain the pasta again.

③ Add the sauce, both cheeses, and the garlic butter to a large, heavy-bottomed pot and cook over medium heat. Stir until the cheese is barely melted, about 3 minutes. Slowly add the cooked pasta, stir, and continue cooking while stirring continuously until the dish is nice and hot, another 5 minutes.

④ Spoon into bowls and serve hot.

International Relations

RECIPES FROM AROUND THE WORLD

Like many California restaurateurs, we wanted to focus on using as many local cheeses as possible when we first opened Homeroom. We liked the idea of supporting local producers and making local food accessible, affordable, and unfussy. However, we knew that we would be remiss to ignore all the amazing international cheeses out there, and so we invented the Exchange Student.

Homeroom's version is an edible take on the cultural insights (and maybe a surprising tradition or two) that a high school exchange student brings along—in the form of a monthly rotating dish featuring unique cheeses and exotic flavors. Our first was the Cacio e Pepe—a Roman version of mac and cheese that features pecorino cheese and cracked black pepper (you can find it on page 46). It was so popular that our customers screamed when we tried to rotate it off the menu. Instead, it stayed there a whole year and even after we pulled it off the printed menu we put it on our secret menu so regulars in-the-know could still get their fix.

Because of the rampant popularity of the Exchange Student, we rarely get to change it out as we had intended. Many of the recipes in this chapter have yet to even hit the Homeroom menu—so you at home will be the first to get to try them. We hope it gives you the chance to play with some new cheeses, and feel like you had an exchange student in your kitchen for a night.

MACXIMUS

We modeled this dish on the addictive Greek pastry spanakopita. When we thought of doing a Greek mac, we could think of nothing more delectable than mimicking this crispy pastry filled with spinach and feta. With spinach, artichoke hearts, shallots, and three different cheeses, our version tastes remarkably like the spanakopita filling, and we bake it in the oven to give it a crispy topping. **Serves 4**

1/2 pound dried elbow pasta

1 cup crumbled feta cheese

1/2 cup grated Jack cheese

1/2 cup grated pecorino cheese

2 teaspoons minced shallots

1/2 cup thawed frozen chopped spinach, thoroughly drained

1/2 cup canned artichoke hearts, drained

2 cups Mac Sauce (page 9)

1/2 cup panko (Japanese bread crumbs)

BEER PAIRING: Amber or Brown Ale

WINE PAIRING: Syrah or Viognier

LESSON PLAN

1. Cook the pasta in salted boiling water until a little less than al dente. Drain, rinse with cold water, and drain the pasta again.

2. Preheat the oven to 400°F. Add the feta, Jack, pecorino, shallots, spinach, artichokes, and sauce to a large, heavy-bottomed pan over medium heat. Stir until the cheeses begin to melt, about 4 minutes (the feta will not melt—so you are just looking for the pecorino and Jack to melt and the mixture to get hot).

3. Slowly add the cooked pasta and stir until hot. Pour into a 12-inch baking dish and top with the panko. Bake until bubbly, 10 to 15 minutes.

4. Spoon into bowls and serve hot.

THE GREEK MAC!

CROQUE MADAME MAC

France's version of a toasted ham and cheese sandwich is known as a croque monsieur. When topped with a fried egg, croque monsieur morphs into its decadent cousin—croque madame. This mac is our version of the tasty French treat found in cafés all over the country. We loved the idea of a gooey ham and cheese mac with a crispy panko crust and topped with a fried egg.

Thinking that more is more—our favorite way to make this is in individual soufflé dishes or large ramekins, and to top each one with a fried egg. However, you can also just bake this in a large casserole dish and decide whether you'd like a single fried egg on top, or if you'd like each person to have their own fried egg (in which case, make enough for everyone). **Serves 4**

1/2 pound dried elbow pasta

1 cup grated Swiss cheese

1 cup grated Jack cheese

1 cup diced ham

2 cups Mac Sauce (page 9)

1 tablespoon fresh tarragon

1/2 cup panko (Japanese bread crumbs)

4 tablespoons butter or oil

4 large eggs

BEER PAIRING: Belgian Ale or Dry Cider

WINE PAIRING: Beaujolais or Rosé

LESSON PLAN

1. Preheat the oven to 400°F.

2. Cook the pasta in salted boiling water until a little less than al dente. Drain, rinse with cold water, and drain the pasta again.

3. Add the cheeses, ham, and sauce to a large, heavy-bottomed pot and cook over medium heat. Stir until the cheeses are barely melted and the ingredients are mixed together, about 3 minutes. Slowly add the cooked pasta, stirring until coated, and add the tarragon.

4. Spoon the mac into 4 individual ovenproof soufflé dishes or large ramekins, or into a large 12-inch ovenproof casserole. Top with panko, and cook in the oven until bubbly around the edges, about 10 minutes.

⑤ Meanwhile, fry the eggs while the mac is in the oven: Heat 2 tablespoons of the butter in a large sauté pan or skillet over medium-high heat. Crack 2 of the eggs into the pan, cover, and let cook undisturbed for about 2 minutes—they should be cooked only long enough for the whites to be set, but the yolks still runny. Slide the eggs onto a plate and repeat with the remaining 2 tablespoons butter and 2 eggs.

⑥ When the macs emerge from the oven, place 1 fried egg on top of each individual ramekin, or, if cooked in the large casserole, spoon the mac into bowls and top each with a fried egg.

THE FRENCH MAC!

CACIO E PEPE

The Italians (Romans, specifically) mastered their own version of cheesy noodles long ago with Cacio e Pepe (pronounced "kah-choh ee pe-pe"). It's as simple as salt and pepper. Pecorino Romano, lots of cracked black peppercorns, and, in our case, mixed with the magical Mac Sauce. This mac was the first "exchange student" on the Homeroom menu, and even though we planned to change up the dish, it secured a permanent place because our customers just wouldn't let us take it off. **Serves 4**

1/2 pound dried elbow pasta

2 cups Mac Sauce (page 9)

1 cup grated Pecorino Romano cheese

1 cup grated Jack cheese

1 1/2 tablespoons whole black peppercorns, crushed

BEER PAIRING: Black Lager

WINE PAIRING: Barbera

LESSON PLAN

① Cook the pasta in salted boiling water until a little less than al dente. Drain, rinse with cold water, and drain the pasta again.

② Add the sauce, cheeses, and crushed peppercorns to a large, heavy-bottomed pot and cook over medium heat. Stir until the cheese is barely melted, about 3 minutes. Slowly add the cooked pasta, stir, and continue cooking while stirring continuously until the dish is nice and hot, another 5 minutes.

③ Spoon into bowls and enjoy.

THE ITALIAN MAC!

MEXICAN MAC

The Mexican Mac was one of the first recipes we developed for Homeroom. Before the restaurant opened, we spent months in our home kitchens grating cheeses, testing spices, cooking vegetables, and eating more mac and cheese than you can imagine. Some people thought we were crazy. "Really?" they would say. "You think you can sustain an entire restaurant based only on mac and cheese?"

We knew we would prove them wrong. Especially when we mastered a recipe as delicious as the Mexican mac. It resembles our favorite taco: spicy pork, tangy cheese, a sprinkle of cilantro, and a big squeeze of fresh lime. And like we tell everyone at Homeroom who orders it, the lime really does make the dish. You can find chipotles en adobo in the international section of most supermarkets. Chipotles are actually dried and smoked jalapeño peppers, and you'll usually find them swimming in a tangy tomato sauce called adobo. Since you don't need the entire can for this recipe, we suggest storing it in the fridge and mixing it with a bit of mayo to spread on sandwiches, tacos, grilled chicken, or anything else that needs a little kick. **Serves 4**

1/2 pound dried elbow pasta

1/2 pound Mexican chorizo (if your chorizo has a casing, remove it before cooking)

1 (7-ounce) can chipotle chiles en adobo

2 cups Mac Sauce (page 9)

2 cups grated Jack cheese

1 bunch cilantro, stemmed and leaves chopped, for garnish

1 lime, cut into wedges, for accompaniment

BEER PAIRING: IPA

WINE PAIRING: Malbec or Tempranillo

LESSON PLAN

1. Cook the pasta in salted boiling water until a little less than al dente. Drain, rinse with cold water, and drain the pasta again.

2. Cook the chorizo in a large sauté pan over medium-high heat, breaking it up with a wooden spoon as it cooks. It will be completely browned when cooked through, about 7 minutes. After it's cooked, let the chorizo drain on a plate lined with a paper towel.

3. Meanwhile, remove the whole chipotles from the can and chop them finely. Mix the chopped chipotles with the adobo sauce from the can.

④ Add the sauce and Jack cheese to a large, heavy-bottomed pot and cook over medium heat. Stir until the cheese is barely melted, about 3 minutes. Slowly add the cooked chorizo and 1/4 cup of the chipotle mixture, then the cooked pasta. Continue cooking while stirring continuously until the dish is nice and hot, another 5 minutes.

⑤ Spoon into bowls and top each with a generous sprinkling of cilantro. Serve with a wedge of lime.

SRIRACHA MAC

It is *hard* to make an Asian-inspired mac and cheese. But after all our experimental failures (think sweet chili sauce and pork mac . . . eww), we had our aha! moment when we thought to blast a mac with that wildly popular fiery red rooster sauce. If you're the kind of person who douses everything with sriracha, this mac is for you. You're welcome! **Serves 4**

1/2 pound dried elbow pasta

1 tablespoon minced fresh ginger

2 1/2 tablespoons unsalted butter, at room temperature

2 cups Mac Sauce (page 9)

2 cups grated Havarti cheese

2 tablespoons sriracha sauce, plus more for drizzling

1 cup chopped green onions (green and light green parts only)

1/2 cup panko (Japanese bread crumbs)

BEER PAIRING: Pale Ale

WINE PAIRING: Sparkling White Wine

LESSON PLAN

1. Preheat the oven to 400°F.

2. Cook the pasta in salted boiling water until a little less than al dente. Drain, rinse with cold water, and drain the pasta again.

3. Mash together the ginger and butter in a small bowl until fully combined.

4. Add the sauce, cheese, and ginger butter to a large, heavy-bottomed pot and cook over medium heat. Stir until the cheese is barely melted, about 3 minutes. Add the sriracha and the cooked pasta, and continue cooking while stirring continuously until the dish is nice and hot, another 5 minutes. Add the green onions and stir to fully combine.

5. Pour the mac into a 14-inch casserole pan and sprinkle with panko. Bake until hot and bubbly and the topping is golden, about 20 minutes. Remove from the oven and drizzle with more sriracha.

6. Spoon into bowls and serve.

THE SOUTHEAST ASIAN MAC!

SHEPHERD'S MAC

We don't use many different kinds of meat at Homeroom. We have an unusually small kitchen for a restaurant, meaning our refrigeration space is extremely limited. So when we started writing this cookbook, we were super-excited to experiment with a whole slew of ingredients that just wouldn't work in our cramped kitchen.

There's only one thing that can possibly be more comforting than Shepherd's Pie, and that's Shepherd's Pie topped with mac and cheese—layers of ground beef, sautéed veggies, and creamy mac, topped with panko and baked until gooey and bubbling. The Brits were definitely on to something when they created this savory pie. It's too bad they missed out on the best part: the mac. **Serves 4**

1/2 pound dried elbow pasta

3/4 pound ground beef

Kosher salt

1 cup chopped onion

1 cup chopped carrots

1 cup frozen peas, thawed and drained

2 cups Mac Sauce (page 9)

2 cups grated aged, sharp English Cheddar cheese

1/2 cup panko (Japanese bread crumbs)

BEER PAIRING: Nutty Brown Ale

WINE PAIRING: Rhône Blend

LESSON PLAN

1. Cook the pasta in salted boiling water until a little less than al dente. Drain, rinse with cold water, and drain the pasta again.

2. Add the ground beef to a large sauté pan and season with 1 tablespoon of kosher salt. Cook over medium heat, breaking the meat into small pieces with a wooden spoon, until cooked through and no longer pink, about 10 minutes. Using a slotted spoon, transfer the meat to a large bowl.

3. Add the onion and carrots to the sauté pan and cook in the fat rendered from the ground beef, stirring occasionally, over medium heat until softened, about 5 minutes. Add the peas, and continue cooking for another 3 to 4 minutes. Add the veggies to the bowl with the meat and stir to combine.

4. Preheat the oven to 400°F.

CONTINUED

⑤ Add the sauce and cheese to a large, heavy-bottomed pot and cook over medium heat. Stir until the cheese is barely melted, about 3 minutes. Slowly add the cooked pasta, stir, and continue cooking while stirring continuously until the dish is nice and hot, another 5 minutes.

⑥ Spread the ground beef–veggie mixture in a 14-inch casserole pan. Spoon on the mac and cheese in an even layer, and finish with a layer of panko. Bake until bubbly and the topping is golden brown, about 15 minutes.

⑦ Spoon into bowls and serve hot.

THE BRITISH MAC!

Minty, Buttery Peas
(page 88)

DELICIOUSMÄCKEN

About twice a year, we have a recipe-testing day at Homeroom, when we invite our entire staff to join us in the kitchen and help create new macs for the coming season. It's an awesome event. Everyone brings ingredients and cheeses they'd like to play with, and we discover some incredible combinations—like this German mac with pretzel topping. Then, we sit down to a feast of new mac and cheeses.

When shopping for mustard, get one that's whole grain—where you can actually see the seeds floating around in the dark yellow mustard. These mustards have a much stronger mustardy flavor than plain yellow mustard, which usually tastes more like vinegar. You'll appreciate that intense mustard flavor even more when it's mixed into a mac and cheese and topped with pretzels. **Serves 4**

2 tablespoons unsalted butter

1 large white onion, thinly sliced

1 teaspoon kosher salt

1/2 pound dried elbow pasta

2 cups Mac Sauce (page 9)

2 tablespoons whole grain mustard

1 1/2 cups grated aged horseradish Cheddar cheese

1/2 cup grated mild Cheddar cheese

1 cup crushed salted pretzels

BEER PAIRING: Hefeweizen

WINE PAIRING: Gewürztraminer

LESSON PLAN

① Melt the butter over medium heat in a large sauté pan. Add the onion and salt, and stir to coat. Cook the onion until browned and caramelized, about 20 minutes, giving it a stir every once in a while. Set aside.

② Cook the pasta in salted boiling water until a little less than al dente. Drain, rinse with cold water, and drain the pasta again.

③ Add the sauce, mustard, and cheeses to a large, heavy-bottomed pot and cook over medium heat. Stir until the cheese is barely melted, about 3 minutes. Slowly add the caramelized onion and the cooked pasta. Continue cooking while stirring continuously until the dish is nice and hot, another 5 minutes.

④ Spoon into bowls, top with crushed pretzels, and serve.

THE GERMAN MAC!

IT'S GOUDA!

Age matters when it comes to cheese, and even more so when it comes to Gouda. Young Gouda is mellow, creamy, and buttery. A couple of years later, it becomes harder, and much more intense. On their own, neither type worked very well for this mac. But mix the two together, and it's just right. We throw in some homemade croutons and think of this as the "fondue mac," even though fondue is originally from Switzerland. You can also add broccoli, carrots, or even sliced apple. Pretty much anything that you'd want to dip into a fondue pot would be extra-tasty when added to the Gouda mac. **Serves 4**

1/2 baguette (preferably day-old), cut into 1/2-inch cubes

1 tablespoon extra-virgin olive oil

Kosher salt

1/2 pound dried elbow pasta

2 cups Mac Sauce (page 9)

1 cup grated aged, hard Gouda

1 cup grated young, soft Gouda

1 tablespoon dry white wine

BEER PAIRING: Hefeweizen

WINE PAIRING: Chardonnay

LESSON PLAN

① Preheat the oven to 350°F.

② Spread the bread cubes on a baking sheet, drizzle with the olive oil, and sprinkle with salt. Use your hands to mix the croutons with the oil and salt to coat evenly. Bake until the bread is crunchy and golden, about 10 minutes. Set aside.

③ Cook the pasta in salted boiling water until a little less than al dente. Drain, rinse with cold water, and drain the pasta again.

④ Add the sauce, cheeses, and wine to a large, heavy-bottomed pot and cook over medium heat. Stir until the cheese is barely melted, about 3 minutes. Slowly add the cooked pasta, stir, and continue cooking while stirring continuously until the dish is nice and hot, about 5 minutes.

⑤ Mix half of the croutons into the mac and cheese, and pour into a serving dish. Spread the remaining croutons on top, spoon into bowls, and enjoy.

THE NETHERLANDS MAC!

PATATAS BRAVAS MAC

The complex flavors of smoked paprika, garlic, and lemon juice make this the mac to make when you want to impress some friends. Like Pecorino Romano and Asiago, Spanish Manchego is a sheep's milk cheese—it is creamy, salty, and hardens as it ages. Look for Manchego that's at least six months old. And while you're cooking the spicy red sauce and gently frying thin slices of potatoes, feel free to whip up a story or two about that time you spent in Spain, sipping cocktails and enjoying tapas on the beach in Barcelona. Wait, that didn't really happen? Oh well. No one needs to know. **Serves 4**

1/2 pound dried elbow pasta

2 tablespoons olive oil

3 fingerling potatoes, thinly sliced, skin on

2 tablespoons butter, at room temperature

1 tablespoon smoked paprika

2 cloves garlic, minced

2 tablespoons freshly squeezed lemon juice

Kosher salt

2 cups Mac Sauce (page 9)

2 cups grated 6-month-aged Manchego cheese

BEER PAIRING: Amber Lager

WINE PAIRING: Tempranillo

LESSON PLAN

1. Cook the pasta in salted boiling water until a little less than al dente. Drain, rinse with cold water, and drain the pasta again.

2. Line a plate with paper towels and have nearby. Heat the olive oil in a sauté pan over medium heat, and cook the potato slices until lightly golden, about 6 minutes. Transfer the slices to the towel-lined plate to drain.

3. Combine the butter, smoked paprika, garlic, lemon juice, and 1 teaspoon of the salt in a small bowl. Mash together into a thick paste.

4. Add the sauce, paprika paste, and cheese to a large, heavy-bottomed pot and cook over medium heat. Stir until the cheese is barely melted, about 3 minutes. Slowly add the cooked pasta, stir, and continue cooking while stirring continuously until the dish is nice and hot, another 5 minutes.

5. Spoon into bowls and arrange the potato slices in a single layer on top of each portion. Serve right away.

THE SPANISH MAC!

CHEMISTRY

EXPERIMENTS WITH UNUSUAL INGREDIENTS

When the right elements come together, magical things happen. Hydrogen and oxygen, for example, give us water. And when truffles combine with a delicious, creamy Gouda, you get an equally impressive result: Truffle Mac (page 63).

We love combining unique ingredients and stinky cheeses to create over-the-top mac and cheese dishes. Much like chemistry class, though, if you're experimenting with cheeses and not obeying a few basic rules, you'll end up with very disappointing results (but you probably won't set your lab partner's hair on fire).

The most important thing to remember is that strong flavors go a long way. You may love blue cheese, but if you don't mix it with a mild cheese when you add it to a mac, it's overwhelming and almost inedible.

Some of Homeroom's most popular dishes fall into the Chemistry category: Vegan (page 62), Mac and Blue (page 68), and Mac the Goat (page 67). So play around with some of your favorite foods—you never know when you'll invent something magical.

FOUR-CHEESE MAC

We're guessing you like cheese. Why else would you be reading this book, right? But if you're like us, you *really* like cheese. We start every meal with a cheese plate, order extra cheese on our pizzas, and seek out fancy cheese stores every time we travel.

So we decided to test the maximum amount of cheese that can go into a mac and cheese, and came up with the cheesiest, gooiest dish we make. You can experiment with lots of cheese combinations, but follow a few rules to ensure you get the tastiest mac possible:

1. Don't use more than one intense, moldy cheese, like a gorgonzola or blue.
2. Don't use more than one salty, hard cheese, like Parmigiano-Reggiano, Pecorino Romano, or Manchego.
3. Mind your proportions: use more of the mild cheeses, and less of the strong cheeses.

A note on mozzarella: It's great on pizza, but a little tricky to use in mac and cheese. If it melts all the way, your sauce will get stringy—not the good kind of stringy; it'll all stick together and become difficult to eat. So cut it in 1-inch cubes and add it after you turn off the heat. That way you'll get delicious chunks of gooeyness instead of a stringy mess.

And that's it. Now go play with some cheese. **Serves 4**

1/2 pound dried elbow pasta

2 cups Mac Sauce (page 9)

2/3 cup grated provolone cheese

1/2 cup crumbled gorgonzola cheese

1/2 cup grated pecorino cheese

2/3 cup cubed fresh mozzarella cheese

1 cup chopped fresh flat-leaf parsley

BEER PAIRING: Crisp Pilsner

WINE PAIRING: Pinot Grigio

LESSON PLAN

1. Cook the pasta in salted boiling water until a little less than al dente. Drain, rinse with cold water, and drain the pasta again.

2. Add the sauce, provolone, gorgonzola, and pecorino to a large, heavy-bottomed pot and cook over medium heat. Stir until the cheese is barely melted, about 3 minutes. Slowly add the cooked pasta, stir, and continue cooking while stirring continuously until the dish is nice and hot, another 5 minutes. Add the mozzarella and the parsley and stir to combine.

3. Spoon into bowls and serve.

SPRING MAC

You know that feeling you get on the first warm, sunny day of the year? We captured that feeling, and topped it with cheese. The Spring Mac is light, refreshing, and just the thing you want when you're sitting out on a sunny patio sipping some bubbly (or when you wish you were).

The secret ingredient is the gremolata, which is simply a fancy word for chopped up herbs and lemon zest. You can add gremolata to just about anything for a fresh dose of spring. Try it in scrambled eggs, on grilled chicken, or with anything else that needs a little brightening up. When you're preparing the gremolata, try using a Microplane food grater to zest the lemon. A Microplane grates super-finely, which helps release all the bright oils from the citrus peel. **Serves 4**

1/2 pound dried elbow pasta

GREMOLATA

3 tablespoons grated lemon zest

1/3 cup finely chopped fresh flat-leaf parsley leaves

1/3 cup finely chopped fresh mint leaves

2 cups Mac Sauce (page 9)

1 1/2 cups grated aged Asiago cheese

1/2 cup grated Jack cheese

1 1/2 cups frozen peas, thawed

Lemon wedges, for serving

BEER PAIRING: Belgian Witbier

WINE PAIRING: Prosecco

LESSON PLAN

1. Cook the pasta in salted boiling water until a little less than al dente. Drain, rinse with cold water, and drain the pasta again.

2. To make the gremolata: Stir together the lemon zest, parsley, and mint in a small bowl. Set aside.

3. Add the sauce and cheeses to a large, heavy-bottomed pot and cook over medium heat. Stir until the cheeses are barely melted, about 3 minutes. Slowly add the peas, gremolata, and cooked pasta. Stir, and continue cooking while stirring continuously until the dish is nice and hot, another 5 minutes.

4. Spoon into bowls, garnish with wedges of lemon, and serve.

VEGAN MAC

We know how this sounds. It defies logic. It goes against all the lessons we have taught you so far—a mac and cheese with no cheese?! Lest you think this recipe is not for you, let us tell you about all of the devoted fans of everything meat and cheese who come into Homeroom and order the vegan, but add bacon, chorizo, or hot dog to it. That's right, this sauce is that good.

We don't like messing with soy products that are flavored to taste like meat, or "cheeses" that are somehow engineered to melt without having any dairy. So for our vegan mac, we use nutritional yeast to get a nutty, cheesy flavor, and soy sauce for an intense, earthy saltiness. Don't knock it until you try it! Nutritional yeast is a deactivated yeast, so it won't make bread and pastries rise like baker's yeast. It has tons of good stuff in it, like protein, folic acid, and vitamin B_{12}. You can find it in the bulk section of most grocery stores. **Serves 4**

1/2 pound dried elbow pasta

1/2 cup water

8 ounces firm tofu

1/2 cup canola oil

1 cup unsweetened soy milk

1/4 cup soy sauce

1 cup nutritional yeast

1 1/2 teaspoons paprika

1 1/2 teaspoons garlic powder

1 teaspoon kosher salt

1/2 cup crushed toasted walnuts (see page 68)

BEER PAIRING: Porter

WINE PAIRING: Cabernet Sauvignon

LESSON PLAN

1. Cook the pasta in salted boiling water until a little less than al dente. Drain, rinse with cold water, and drain the pasta again.

2. To make the vegan sauce: Put the water, tofu, oil, soy milk, soy sauce, nutritional yeast, paprika, garlic powder, and salt in a blender and puree until smooth.

3. Add the vegan sauce and the cooked pasta to a large, heavy-bottomed pot, stir, and cook over medium heat until the dish is nice and hot, about 5 minutes.

4. Spoon into bowls, top with the crushed walnuts, and serve.

TRUFFLE MAC

The first year Homeroom was open, we threw a New Year's Eve party for people who hate New Year's Eve parties. It was casual, inexpensive, and had lots of awesome food. We choose three macs and paired them with three different wines and beers, and everyone got to enjoy as much mac as they could eat. And as a special treat, we debuted a mac that hundreds of customers had been asking for: the Truffle Mac.

Instead of using truffle oil, which is usually made from an assortment of chemicals and doesn't actually contain any truffles, we use an intense cheese that is laced with real black truffles. Most cheese departments will carry at least one kind of truffle cheese. We like the truffle Gouda because along with its intense truffle flavor, it also melts really well.

If you can't find a truffle cheese, try using truffle salt, which also contains real truffles. If you go that route, replace the salt in the mac sauce (as well as any extra salt that you add at the end for seasoning) with the truffle salt. **Serves 4**

1/2 pound dried elbow pasta

2 tablespoons unsalted butter

2 cups sliced shiitake mushrooms

2 cups Mac Sauce (page 9)

2 cups grated truffle Gouda

1 tablespoon fresh thyme leaves

BEER PAIRING: Brown Ale
WINE PAIRING: Dolcetto

LESSON PLAN

1. Cook the pasta in salted boiling water until a little less than al dente. Drain, rinse with cold water, and drain the pasta again.

2. Melt the butter in a large sauté pan, and add the mushrooms. Cook until the mushrooms are soft, about 6 minutes.

3. Add the sauce and cheese to a large, heavy-bottomed pot and cook over medium heat. Stir until the cheese is barely melted, about 3 minutes. Add the mushrooms, fresh thyme, and the cooked pasta, stir, and continue cooking while stirring continuously until the dish is nice and hot, another 5 minutes.

4. Spoon into bowls and enjoy.

DUNGENESS CRAB MAC

One of the questions we get most often from our customers is, "Why don't you have a crab mac on the menu?" To help keep the food at Homeroom accessible to everyone in our community, we price all of our macs around ten dollars or less. And to have a good crab mac, you must use good crabmeat—and that would make one expensive mac.

Although we don't serve this crab mac at the restaurant, it didn't seem fair to hide it from the world entirely. So here it is, tasting like a giant, crispy crab cake on top of gooey, creamy mac and cheese. Ninety-nine percent of the time, we would say to never pair cheese with seafood. If you are going to pair the two together, the trick is to use a mild, buttery cheese that melts well. We used a local Bay Area cheese called Carmody from Bellwether Farms, but you can also get great results with a Havarti. Don't skimp on the crabmeat. It'll be pricey, but worth the expense. **Serves 4**

1/2 pound dried elbow pasta

3 tablespoons unsalted butter

1 yellow onion, coarsely chopped

1 red bell pepper, cored, seeded, and coarsely chopped

1/2 pound cooked crabmeat, picked over for shells

3 teaspoons Old Bay Seasoning

1 teaspoon kosher salt

2 cups Mac Sauce (page 9)

2 cups grated Carmody cheese (or Havarti)

1/2 cup grated Parmesan cheese

1/2 cup panko (Japanese bread crumbs)

1 lemon, cut into wedges

LESSON PLAN

1. Cook the pasta in salted boiling water until a little less than al dente. Drain, rinse with cold water, and drain the pasta again.

2. Preheat the oven to 400°F.

3. Melt the butter in a large sauté pan over medium heat. Add the onion and bell pepper to the pan and cook until they're softened, about 10 minutes. Add the crabmeat, 2 teaspoons of the Old Bay Seasoning, and the 1 teaspoon salt to the pan and cook for another 2 minutes. Turn off the heat and set aside.

4. Add the sauce and Carmody cheese to a large, heavy-bottomed pot and cook over medium heat. Stir until the cheese is barely melted, about 3 minutes. Add the

CONTINUED

DUNGENESS CRAB MAC, CONTINUED

BEER PAIRING: Hefeweizen
with a lemon slice

WINE PAIRING: Pinot Gris

crabmeat mixture and the cooked pasta, stir, and continue cooking while stirring continuously for another 5 minutes.

5. Spoon the mac and cheese into a 14-inch ovenproof casserole. Sprinkle the Parmesan on top and then the panko. Lastly, sprinkle on the remaining 1 teaspoon of Old Bay Seasoning. Bake until golden and bubbly, about 15 minutes.

6. Spoon into serving bowls and serve with lemon wedges.

MAC THE GOAT

With tangy chèvre, sliced green onions, and a drizzle of olive oil, this is one of our lighter and more refreshing macs. The trick to using chèvre (goat's milk cheese) in mac and cheese is heating it over low heat. When any cheese is heated over high heat, it will break and become grainy—but goat cheese is particularly sensitive. We recommend cooking it over low heat to give the cheese time to slowly melt without losing its creamy texture. Also, Mac the Goat is the one mac in this book that *must* be baked. Because goat cheese has more water than other cheeses, the sauce is a bit runnier. To remedy this, we bake it in the oven with panko bread crumbs on top to bring it all together. Mac the Goat has been on our menu since opening day, and is a favorite among goat cheese lovers, and those who just love a damn good mac and cheese. **Serves 4**

1/2 pound dried elbow pasta

2 cups Mac Sauce (page 9)

6 ounces fresh goat cheese (chèvre), crumbled

1/2 cup grated Jack cheese

4 green onions (green and light green parts), sliced

1/2 cup panko (Japanese bread crumbs)

2 tablespoons olive oil, for drizzling

BEER PAIRING: Saison

WINE PAIRING: Pinot Noir

LESSON PLAN

1. Preheat the oven to 400°F.

2. Cook the pasta in salted boiling water until a little less than al dente. Drain, rinse with cold water, and drain the pasta again.

3. Add the sauce, goat cheese, Jack cheese, and green onions to a large, heavy-bottomed pot, and cook over low heat until the goat cheese is barely melted, about 3 minutes. Slowly add the cooked pasta and heat just until the pasta is warm while stirring continuously.

4. Spoon the mac into a 14-inch ovenproof casserole, and sprinkle with panko. Bake until bubbly, about 10 minutes.

5. Spoon into bowls, drizzle with olive oil, and serve.

MAC AND BLUE

This is one of our more sophisticated macs, even though it has one of our less sophisticated names (we were trying to make a pun on "black and blue," but no one seems to get it but us). The trouble with blue cheese is how to tame it—it's incredibly pungent and we didn't want a mac that was too overpowering. The trick is to combine a small amount of blue cheese with a large amount of a less aggressive cheese (here, it's Jack), so the blue's flavor permeates the dish but in a more subtle way. We top this mac with toasted walnuts, because blue cheese and walnuts are a natural pairing. We often sell it as a side dish for Thanksgiving, but it can also stand alone as a main dish in the fall, winter—or really any old time. **Serves 4**

1/2 pound dried elbow pasta

1 cup walnuts

2 cups Mac Sauce (page 9)

13/4 cups grated Jack cheese

1/4 cup crumbled blue cheese (we recommend Point Reyes Original Blue, but any will do)

BEER PAIRING: Stout or Porter

WINE PAIRING: Zinfandel

LESSON PLAN

1. Cook the pasta in salted boiling water until a little less than al dente. Drain, rinse with cold water, and drain the pasta again.

2. Toast the walnuts (this brings out their tasty, nutty flavor): Preheat the oven to 350°F. Place the walnuts on a baking sheet and bake the nuts until brown and toasty, 5 to 10 minutes. Alternatively, you can toast the walnuts in a skillet over high heat, stirring them constantly, until they deepen in color and smell toasted, about 3 minutes. The nuts don't toast as evenly on the stove as in the oven, but it's a shortcut. Cool the nuts and chop them into smaller pieces.

3. Add the sauce and the cheeses to a large, heavy-bottomed pot over medium heat. Stir until the cheese is barely melted, about 3 minutes. Slowly add the cooked pasta, stir, and continue cooking over medium heat while stirring continuously until it's nice and hot.

4. Spoon into bowls, top with the walnuts, and serve.

PESTO MAC

The first summer we opened our restaurant, we were worried that if we only served hot, rich, creamy mac and cheese people wouldn't come on really hot days. It turns out that people love a piping bowl of mac and cheese no matter what the weather. A great byproduct of our unfounded fears was that it led us to develop our only cold mac and cheese—the Pesto Mac. Truthfully, this dish isn't very mac and cheesy. Yes, there are macaroni noodles, and there is also cheese—but it definitely doesn't conform to usual notions of mac and cheese. It's really more like a pesto pasta. Many customers like to add a scoop of pesto to another mac and cheese (it is particularly delicious in the Vermont White Cheddar Mac, page 31). So eat it by itself, or scoop it into another mac for an added kick. **Serves 4**

1/2 pound dried elbow pasta or other pasta of your choice

2 or 3 cloves garlic

1/3 cup chopped walnuts

2/3 cup grated pecorino cheese

1/4 cup fresh flat-leaf parsley leaves

4 ounces basil leaves (no stems!)

11/2 cups olive oil

41/2 teaspoons freshly squeezed lemon juice

1/2 tablespoon kosher salt

BEER PAIRING: Summer Ale

WINE PAIRING: Fumé Blanc

LESSON PLAN

1. Cook the pasta in salted boiling water until al dente. If you like cold pesto pasta, drain, rinse with cold water, and drain the pasta again. Then set the pasta aside and let cool. If you want hot pesto pasta, hold off on cooking the pasta until after you have finished making the pesto sauce, then add the pesto to the pasta while it is still warm.

2. In a food processor, pulse together the garlic, walnuts, and pecorino until they look like tiny pebbles.

3. Add the parsley and basil and pulse until the leaves are shredded into very tiny uniform pieces, forming a paste. Transfer to a bowl.

4. With a spatula, stir in the olive oil, lemon juice, and salt. Taste for salt and adjust as needed.

5. Add to hot pasta, cold pasta, or throw a scoop or two into any mac and cheese recipe in this cookbook.

MAC-CAKES
(LIKE PANCAKES, ONLY BETTER)

A surprising number of people have asked us to add fried mac and cheese or mac and cheese pancakes to our menu. We always said no because both sounded more kitschy than tasty. However, when it came time to write this cookbook, we decided that it was at least worth experimenting with these kooky suggestions to see if they were good or gross. Fried mac and cheese was yummy, but it's hard to get much cheesy flavor into fried mac balls—they need a lot of other stuff to bind them so they don't fall apart in the deep fryer. However, mac and cheese pancakes (or Mac-Cakes, as we call them) were actually delicious! The key is the contrast between lots of crispy exterior and gooey interior. Both sides of the Mac-Cake are coated in panko and then griddled with extra butter. Crispy, buttery, and cheesy, these are a decadent treat when you feel like regular mac and cheese just won't do. Another fun element of Mac-Cakes is that you can add your favorite toppings. Drizzle on ketchup for a classic combo, sriracha or other hot sauce for spice, or even another dipping sauce that you think would be complementary. **Serves 4**

1 cup dried small elbow pasta

1/2 cup Mac Sauce (page 9)

1 cup grated cheese (Cheddar is classic, but any other favorite cheese will also work)

1 large egg

1 cup panko (Japanese bread crumbs)

4 tablespoons unsalted butter

DRINK PAIRING: **Mimosas or Bloody Marys**

LESSON PLAN

① Cook the pasta in salted boiling water until a little less than al dente. Drain, rinse with cold water, and drain the pasta again.

② Mix the sauce, cheese, and egg together in a bowl. Add the cooked pasta and stir together until evenly mixed. Place the panko bread crumbs in a separate bowl.

③ Place about 2 tablespoons of the mac mixture in the bowl of panko. Gently roll it around in the panko to form a ball that is fully coated with bread crumbs.

CONTINUED

It is a little hard to work with, but don't worry, it doesn't need to be perfect—it's about to be flattened out into a pancake!

④ Heat a griddle or nonstick skillet over medium heat, and butter the pan generously. Place the ball of mac and cheese on the pan, and press it down with the back of the spatula until it flattens out into a thick pancake (not too thin, or it will break apart). Repeat with enough pancakes spaced at least 1 inch apart to fill the griddle or skillet.

⑤ Cook the pancakes on one side until brown and crispy, about 2 minutes, then flip and cook the other side until brown and crispy, another 2 minutes. Transfer the pancakes from the griddle to a serving plate. Repeat, adding more butter as needed, until all the pancakes have been cooked.

⑥ Eat the pancakes as soon as they are ready for maximum crispiness and cheesy gooeyness.

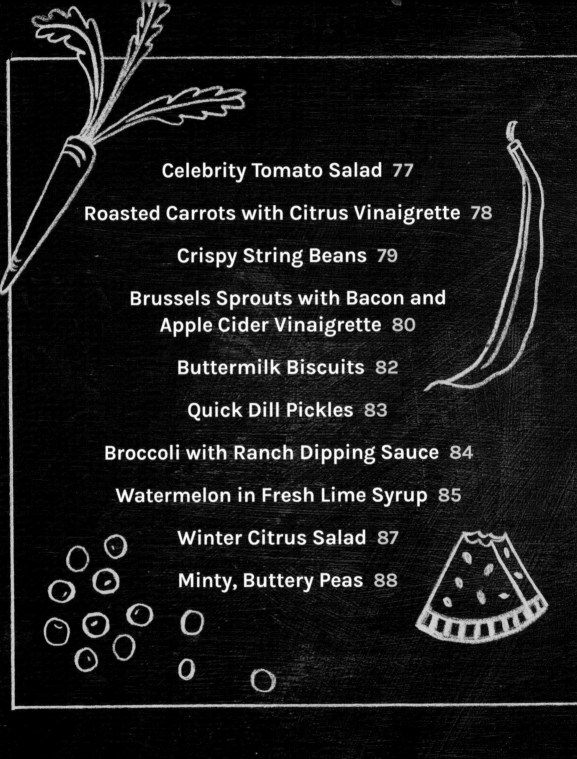

Celebrity Tomato Salad 77

Roasted Carrots with Citrus Vinaigrette 78

Crispy String Beans 79

Brussels Sprouts with Bacon and
Apple Cider Vinaigrette 80

Buttermilk Biscuits 82

Quick Dill Pickles 83

Broccoli with Ranch Dipping Sauce 84

Watermelon in Fresh Lime Syrup 85

Winter Citrus Salad 87

Minty, Buttery Peas 88

Extra Credit

SIDE DISHES

Although we love eating mac and cheese on its own, nothing complements rich, creamy cheeses better than a side of fruit or veggies. These recipes are all super-fast to make, and designed specifically to be paired with any of our mac and cheeses.

We have focused on nostalgic recipes from our childhood that first made eating vegetables fun—like broccoli with ranch dipping sauce (isn't everything more fun with a dipping sauce?). Apparently this approach works, as these dishes are often ordered by the droves of children who eat at Homeroom every day. Many parents have never seen their children scarf down plates of carrots or peas quicker than they do at our restaurant.

But it's not only kids who love eating their veggies at Homeroom. Adults are constantly asking to buy bottles of our sweet and tangy citrus vinaigrette or homemade ranch dressing to turn any vegetable into an addictive snack. Our brussels sprouts with bacon sell out frequently, because even the humble brussels sprout is irresistible when made right. We think the secret is in the preparation. Our sides are simple, casual, and delectable: crunchy carrots, buttery peas, crispy string beans, and more.

CELEBRITY TOMATO SALAD

Here's something you may not have learned in biology class—there are hundreds of heirloom tomato varieties out there, with new ones popping up every year. Some are striped, some are black, some are as small as your pinky nail. And they have funky names like Hillbilly, Mortgage Lifter, Cherokee Purple, and our favorite, Celebrity Tomato.

You can use any of the heirloom varieties for this salad, but it's best to make it when they are in season and ripe. Pair it with a mac for a bright and cheery side dish, or add bites of creamy fresh mozzarella for a bigger, heartier salad that's a meal on its own.

Serves 6

1/2 baguette, cut into 2-inch cubes

4 tablespoons extra-virgin olive oil, plus extra for drizzling

3 pounds heirloom tomatoes

1/2 red onion, halved and thinly sliced

1 cup chopped fresh basil leaves, plus whole leaves for garnish

1 tablespoon balsamic vinegar

1 1/2 teaspoons kosher salt

8 ounces fresh mozzarella, cubed (optional)

LESSON PLAN

1. Preheat the oven to 350°F. Spread out the bread cubes on a baking sheet, and lightly drizzle with olive oil. Bake until golden brown, about 10 minutes; set aside to cool.

2. Halve each tomato along its equator, and halve each section so you have 4 equal pieces. If your tomatoes are large, cut again into eighths. Throw the tomatoes into a large bowl.

3. Rinse the onion slices under cold water and drain. This will remove some of the harshness from the onions. Add to the bowl with the tomatoes.

4. Add the bread cubes, basil, the remaining 4 tablespoons olive oil, balsamic vinegar, salt, and mozzarella cheese to the bowl. Toss to combine. Garnish with several whole basil leaves.

5. Serve right away.

ROASTED CARROTS
WITH CITRUS VINAIGRETTE

Even people who don't like veggies seem to like carrots, and especially our carrots. After roasting, we top them with a citrus vinaigrette made with orange juice, honey, shallots, and Champagne vinegar. The secret to amazing roasted vegetables is to finish them with an acidic dressing to brighten up the veggies' natural flavor.

Sweet and tangy, carrots are the perfect match for rich and creamy mac and cheese. Whip these up easily and quickly, and keep the extra dressing around to add to salads or any other roasted veggie. (See the photo on page 35.) **Serves 4 to 6**

1 pound carrots, cut into 1-inch pieces

1 cup plus 2 tablespoons extra-virgin olive oil

Kosher salt and freshly ground black pepper

1/4 cup freshly squeezed orange juice

1/4 cup Champagne vinegar

2 tablespoons honey

1 tablespoon minced shallots

LESSON PLAN

① Preheat the oven to 400°F.

② Line a baking sheet with aluminum foil. Arrange the carrots in a single layer on the foil. Drizzle with 2 tablespoons of the olive oil, salt and pepper to taste, and toss the carrots to fully coat with oil and seasoning. Bake until tender but not mushy, about 20 minutes.

③ Meanwhile, make the dressing: In a large bowl, add the orange juice, Champagne vinegar, honey, and a pinch of salt and whisk to combine. Add the remaining 1 cup of oil in a slow stream, whisking continuously.

④ When the carrots are finished, throw them in a serving bowl, top with a little dressing, and stir to combine. Eat them hot or cold.

CRISPY STRING BEANS

Green beans are one of the first vegetables we remember eating as children. We'd eat them cooked in butter, covered in tomato sauce, or raw, freshly plucked from a garden.

Blanching the beans first keeps them bright green and crispy. Blanching simply means cooking briefly in boiling water, then plunging in cold water to stop the cooking process. It's the step that was definitely missing any time you were forced to eat mushy, gray, dull beans as a child. Try these beans as is, or instead of sautéing them, let the blanched beans cool down and toss them with our citrus vinaigrette (see opposite). **Serves 4 to 6**

1 pound green beans, stemmed

2 tablespoons salted butter

3 large shallots, thinly sliced

Kosher salt and freshly ground black pepper

LESSON PLAN

① Put on a large pot of water to boil over high heat. Add the green beans and blanch them for about 30 seconds.

② Drain the beans and quickly cool them down by running under cold water. Let drain.

③ Melt the butter in a large sauté pan over medium heat and add the shallots. Cook until soft, about 4 minutes. Add the beans, a sprinkle of salt, and some black pepper. Cook for another 4 minutes.

④ Serve and enjoy!

BRUSSELS SPROUTS
WITH BACON AND APPLE CIDER VINAIGRETTE

Why do these cute little sprouts get such a bad rap? Brussels sprouts are at the top of our list as far as vegetables go—they're hearty, healthy, and even better with bacon.

If it's the bitterness of sprouts that turns you off, this recipe will be a welcome change. Roasting the sprouts and coating them in an apple cider vinaigrette tames any bitter notes. Just ask all the picky children we've seen eating them by the handful. **Serves 4 to 6**

1/2 pound sliced bacon

1 pound brussels sprouts, halved

2 tablespoons extra-virgin olive oil

Kosher salt

2 tablespoons finely chopped shallots

1/4 cup apple cider vinegar

LESSON PLAN

1. Preheat the oven to 400°F.

2. Cook the bacon in a skillet over high heat until crispy, about 8 minutes. Transfer the bacon strips to paper towels to drain, then chop the bacon into bite-size pieces. Pour the residual bacon fat into a bowl.

3. Spread the halved brussels sprouts in a single layer on a baking sheet. Drizzle with the olive oil, sprinkle on some salt, and toss to coat evenly. Roast until lightly browned and crispy, about 20 minutes.

4. Meanwhile, make the vinaigrette: In a medium bowl, combine the shallots, 1/2 cup of the reserved bacon fat, and apple cider vinegar. Whisk to combine.

5. Remove the brussels sprouts from oven and toss with the dressing. Serve hot.

BUTTERMILK BISCUITS

Nonbakers, this recipe is for you! Even if your cookies bake up rock solid and your cakes don't rise an inch, you can make flaky, soft, buttermilk biscuits. The golden rule? Do not overmix. If you gently combine the ingredients only until they barely come together, your biscuits will be light and fluffy every time.

We serve these biscuits on the weekends during brunch, paired with sweet jam, or use them for our egg sandwich that we top with cheese and bacon. They're also great served with butter or honey. **Makes 8 biscuits**

2 cups all-purpose flour

1 tablespoon sugar

1 tablespoon baking powder

1/2 teaspoon kosher salt

8 tablespoons cold, unsalted butter, cut into chunks, plus a little melted butter for brushing the tops

1 cup buttermilk

LESSON PLAN

① Preheat the oven to 450°F. Line a baking sheet with parchment paper.

② Add the flour, sugar, baking powder, and salt to the bowl of a heavy-duty stand mixer fitted with a paddle attachment (or a handheld mixer with a paddle attachment) and combine on low speed. Add the 8 tablespoons cold butter to the flour mixture and mix on low speed until it resembles coarse cornmeal. Add the buttermilk and continue to mix on low speed just until the ingredients come together. Turn the dough out onto a floured surface and pat into a 1-inch-thick round.

③ With a 2-inch cookie cutter, cut out rounds of dough (you can make them as big or as little as you like, though larger sizes will take longer to bake). Transfer the biscuits to the prepared baking sheet, and brush with melted butter.

④ Bake until the tops are golden brown, about 10 minutes. Transfer the biscuits to a rack to cool slightly, until warm.

QUICK DILL PICKLES

This recipe comes from our neighbor, Sandy Der. These pickles are not brined for a long time, so they are somewhere between a fresh cucumber and a dill pickle in flavor and texture. We love them because they are so refreshing, and provide a great contrast when served on the side of mac and cheese. They are also great on their own, and are sure to impress friends who will think you have spent your day pickling cucumbers when all it took was five minutes. Don't worry—we won't tell. **Makes 18 to 20 pickles**

9 tablespoons kosher salt

12 cups cold filtered water

18 to 20 pickling cucumbers, scrubbed

8 cloves garlic, unpeeled and slightly crushed

2 tablespoons pickling spice (optional)

6 bay leaves

1 bunch dill (preferably going to seed)

LESSON PLAN

1. Make a brine by dissolving the kosher salt in the 12 cups cold water.

2. Prepare four 1-quart, wide-mouth jars or one 1-gallon jar by running them through the dishwasher or filling them with boiling water, then pouring out the water.

3. Pack the cucumbers vertically into the jars, making sure they're tightly packed. As the jars are filled, divide the garlic, pickling spice, bay leaves, and dill among them.

4. Fill the jars with brine so that the cucumbers are completely covered. Put a weight (anything heavy and nonreactive that's made out of stainless steel or glass) on top of the pickles to keep them submerged. Cover the jars with a fine mesh cloth or a triple layer of cheesecloth, secured with rubber bands, or loosely with the lids. Store in a cool, dark place for 3 days.

5. After 3 days, taste one. The pickles will ferment in 3 to 6 days. The longer the fermentation, the more sour they'll become. Once the pickles are to your liking, refrigerate them. They're best if enjoyed within 3 weeks.

BROCCOLI WITH RANCH DIPPING SAUCE

We love dips. Good old-fashioned onion dip, artichoke dip, and most of all, ranch dip. They remind us of parties when we were young—or big family gatherings. For the restaurant, we decided it would be a little ridiculous to have multiple vegetable dipping sauces, so we went with our favorite: ranch. Once you make this recipe, you will never return to those gross little powdered packets or the plastic bottles at the supermarket. And if you don't like broccoli, then use it on any other vegetable, or in salad, or on a sandwich (we also use it on our BLT, and it's amazing!). **Serves 4 to 6**

1 head broccoli

RANCH DRESSING

2 cups buttermilk

2 cups mayonnaise

1 1/2 cups sour cream

1/4 cup finely chopped shallots

1/4 cup chopped fresh flat-leaf parsley

1/4 cup chopped fresh cilantro

4 cloves garlic, chopped

1 1/2 tablespoons freshly squeezed lemon juice

1 teaspoon freshly ground black pepper

2 to 4 teaspoons kosher salt

LESSON PLAN

1. Remove the florets and stems of broccoli from the stalk. Separate them into easily grabbable, dippable segments.

2. Heat water to a boil in a large pot over high heat. When the water is boiling, add the broccoli and boil for 2 minutes. Drain, and let the broccoli cool (do not pour cold water on it—you want it to keep cooking as it cools). NOTE: This will give you cooked, but still crunchy broccoli—if you like your broccoli soft you can always cook it more.

3. To make the dressing: In a bowl, mix together all ingredients except the salt to make a creamy mixture. Add the salt, 1 teaspoon at a time, tasting after each addition, until the dressing tastes to your liking.

4. Place the dressing in a serving dish, and the cooled broccoli in another—and serve. Dip the broccoli in the ranch dipping sauce and try to stop yourself from eating the whole thing.

WATERMELON IN FRESH LIME SYRUP

It feels a little ridiculous to even call this a recipe since it consists of three ingredients and takes five minutes to make—but oftentimes the simple things are the best. We soak the watermelon in a refreshing lime syrup, amping up watermelon's deliciously refreshing elements so the fruit bursts in your mouth with a cool, summery sweetness. It makes the perfect counterpoint to a rich mac and cheese on a hot summer day. **Serves 4 to 6**

$1/2$ cup water

$1/2$ cup sugar

Grated zest of 1 large lime (or 2 small ones)

Freshly squeezed juice of 1 large lime (or 2 small ones)

8 cups watermelon cubes (1-inch cubes, with rind removed)

LESSON PLAN

1. Stir together the water and sugar in a small saucepan over high heat just until the sugar melts to make a simple syrup. Pour the syrup into a small bowl and place it in the fridge, uncovered, until the syrup cools.

2. Put the watermelon cubes in a large bowl. Add the lime zest and lime juice to the cooled syrup, and pour over the watermelon. Gently stir to coat all the watermelon pieces with the syrup.

3. Serve immediately or store in the refrigerator for up to 4 hours.

WINTER CITRUS SALAD

We both make this salad at home all winter long. Crunchy marinated shallots (you can use an onion if you can't find shallots) contrast with creamy avocado and tangy citrus in this incredibly beautiful and refreshing salad. It is a showstopper if you are having people over, and still very simple and fun to make. **Serves 4**

3 shallots (or 1 onion)

1/4 cup red wine vinegar

1/4 cup apple cider vinegar

1/4 cup sugar

4 oranges, peeled

2 ripe avocados

Extra-virgin olive oil (use your best stuff here!), for drizzling

Coarse sea salt or kosher salt

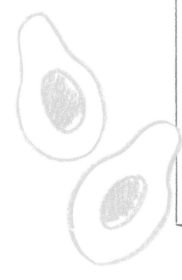

LESSON PLAN

1. Peel the shallots and slice them into very thin strips. In a small bowl, mix together the red wine vinegar, apple cider vinegar, and sugar until the sugar is dissolved. Add the shallot strips to the vinegar mixture, and set aside in the refrigerator for at least 1 hour, and up to 1 day. (This will allow the shallots time to pick up the sweet and tangy flavors of the vinegar mixture, and mellow any harsh flavors in the shallots.)

2. Slice the oranges crosswise (not from stem to blossom end), so that you see the entire cross-section of the orange—not so that the sections naturally separate.

3. Peel and pit the avocados. Cut the avocados into thin slices.

4. To serve, arrange the orange slices on a platter, and then scatter avocado strips across them. Drain the shallots (discard the vinegar marinade unless you want to add a little before serving), and scatter them across the oranges and avocados. Drizzle with olive oil, and sprinkle with coarse sea salt or kosher salt. Serve immediately.

MINTY, BUTTERY PEAS

This is a simple but delicious five-minute side dish. Buttery, salty, and with a hint of mint—these are peas like mama used to make when you were a little kid. A funny story about this dish is that we get asked all the time how we have time to shuck so many fresh peas every day. We use frozen peas, but something about the mint makes them taste so fresh and springlike that everyone assumes we use fresh peas straight from the vine. Minty peas are a great side dish for kids and adults alike, and a perfect way to throw something green on the table when you are short on time. (See the photo on page 53.) **Serves 4**

2 cups frozen peas

2 tablespoons unsalted butter

1/2 teaspoon kosher salt

2 tablespoons chopped fresh mint

LESSON PLAN

① Thaw the peas by placing them in a glass bowl in the microwave for 1 minute or by leaving them out on the counter for about 1 hour before cooking.

② In a saucepan, melt the butter over medium heat. Add the peas and salt and stir until the peas are coated in butter and hot, about 3 minutes.

③ Place in a serving dish, and sprinkle with the chopped mint. Add more mint if you like your peas really minty!

Banana Cream Pie 92

Carrot Cake with
Cream Cheese Frosting 94

Peanut Butter Pie 96

Melted Chocolate Bar Hot Chocolate
with Mint Whipped Cream 98

Dessert Mac 100

Buckeyes 101

Strawberry Crisp 103

Lime Bars 104

Grasshopper Pie with
Homemade Chocolate Sauce 105

Homemade Oreos 107

Best-Ever Brownies 109

FINALS

DESSERTS

Homeroom is a mac and cheese restaurant, but it is almost as famous for its homemade desserts as it is for cheesy noodles. These desserts have won awards, been written up in multiple publications, and most importantly, have a devoted following who (somehow) manage to always save room for them when visiting the restaurant.

What makes our desserts so special is that they weren't developed with a restaurant in mind—they are recipes we grew up with or family recipes from friends and neighbors. They are simple, time-tested, and nostalgic recipes that taste authentic because they are.

The best part is that they are all easy to make. None of the recipes requires fancy equipment, and they are approachable even to those without baking know-how. We are excited to bring these recipes from our restaurant into your home, and know they will bring a delirious smile to your face in the way that only a truly decadent treat can.

BANANA CREAM PIE

Banana cream pie—silky, delicious, and the way we do it—is surprisingly simple. You don't even need a pie tin—we make ours in mason jars so that you can see each beautiful layer. We came upon the concept of "pie in a jar" purely by accident—Erin's sister Alexis was visiting and decided to make a special banana cream pie one night at Homeroom. Although Alexis is a fabulous baker, her crust on that day was a disaster. Instead of throwing it out, she took a mason jar we serve beer in and layered the pie components in the jar instead of in the pie shell. Customers loved it, and so did we—so we tweaked the recipe and put it on the regular menu where it has been one of our best-selling desserts ever since.

We make our banana cream pie as it is often made in the South—using vanilla wafers instead of a traditional pie crust, and layered with a creamy vanilla custard and sliced banana. We recommend making this dessert ahead of time and letting it sit for a few hours before serving it. This way the custard permeates the wafer layers and creates a moist, crumbly, and addictive crust. **Serves 6**

5 cups whole milk

1 cup heavy cream

1/2 cup cornstarch

4 large egg yolks

1 cup sugar

2 tablespoons pure vanilla extract

2 large bananas, peeled and cut crosswise into 1/4-inch slices

18 to 24 vanilla wafers

LESSON PLAN

1. To make the custard: In a large heavy-bottomed pot, combine 4 cups of the milk and the cream over medium heat. In a bowl, whisk together the remaining 1 cup of milk, the cornstarch, egg yolks, sugar, and vanilla.

2. When the milk mixture begins to simmer, add the cornstarch mixture and whisk rapidly. Continue stirring over medium heat until it gets noticeably thicker. Immediately remove it from the heat and pour into a large bowl. Let the mixture cool at room temperature for an hour or more (it gets thicker as it cools)—you can store it covered for up to 2 days in the fridge if you want to make it ahead.

③ To assemble the pies: In six 8-ounce mason jars, layer 2 or 3 vanilla wafers, 2 or 3 banana slices, and 1/2 cup of vanilla custard. Repeat until you have filled each jar.

④ Cover each mason jar with a metal jar lid and band, then place them in the fridge for a few hours or overnight, then serve. This way, the custard seeps into the vanilla wafers and turns them into a soft, delicious layer. Leaving the jars in the fridge also allows more time for the pudding to set and become thicker. If you don't have the time to do this step, you can serve it immediately, but the pudding won't come together quite as well.

CARROT CAKE
WITH CREAM CHEESE FROSTING

This is the only dessert on our menu that we did not invent ourselves; it comes from the family archives of our regular customer Delaney Anderson. This recipe has been in Delaney's family for many years, and is hands-down the best carrot cake we have ever had. She allows us to serve her family secret at Homeroom, and our customers are obsessed with the super-moist cake, slathered with a soft, sweet cream cheese frosting. We are drooling just writing about it. **Makes one 9 by 13-inch cake**

CARROT CAKE

2 cups granulated sugar

2 cups all-purpose flour

2 teaspoons baking soda

2 teaspoons ground cinnamon

1 teaspoon salt

1 cup vegetable oil

4 large eggs, lightly beaten

1 (8-ounce) can crushed pineapple, drained

1/2 cup chopped pecans (optional)

4 cups grated carrots (about 4 large carrots)

LESSON PLAN

1. To make the cake: Preheat the oven to 325°F. Grease and flour a 9 by 13-inch glass baking dish.

2. In a large bowl, sift together the granulated sugar, flour, baking soda, cinnamon, and salt. Add the oil and stir.

3. Add the eggs to the flour mixture and stir with a wooden spoon to blend. Add the pineapple and nuts and stir. Add the carrots last.

4. Pour into the prepared baking dish. Bake until a knife inserted into the center comes out without batter clinging to it, about 45 minutes. (This cake is extremely moist, so a tester will probably not come out completely free of crumbs—but what you are looking for is no uncooked batter on the knife.)

CREAM CHEESE FROSTING

8 ounces regular cream
cheese, at room temperature

6 tablespoons unsalted
butter, at room temperature

3 cups confectioners' sugar

1 teaspoon pure vanilla
extract

⑤ While the cake is baking, make the frosting: In a heavy-duty stand mixer fitted with the paddle attachment (or with a handheld electric mixer), cream together the cream cheese and butter. Slowly sift in the confectioners' sugar and continue beating until there are no lumps. Stir in the vanilla. Let the frosting sit at room temperature until the cake is ready to frost.

⑥ Remove the cake from the oven and let cool on a wire rack. Frost the cake when it is cool. Cut into generous squares and serve.

PEANUT BUTTER PIE

This pie is inspired by the deliciously addictive filling of the magical childhood treat—the peanut butter cup. It almost perfectly mimics its flavor, but with a creamy richness and silky texture that kicks the butt of the original. You can also drizzle on our chocolate sauce (page 105) for extra tastiness. **Makes one 9-inch pie**

1¼ cups graham cracker crumbs

3 tablespoons unsalted butter, melted

1 cup heavy cream

8 ounces cream cheese, at room temperature

1¼ cups creamy peanut butter

¾ cup packed light brown sugar

2 tablespoons pure vanilla extract

LESSON PLAN

① Preheat the oven to 350°F.

② In a bowl, stir together the graham cracker crumbs and melted butter; press into the bottom and sides of a 9-inch pie dish. Bake until brown, about 5 minutes. Set aside to cool completely.

③ With a heavy-duty stand mixer fitted with the whisk attachment, whisk the cream at high speed until it forms stiff peaks. Transfer to a large clean bowl and set aside.

④ Fit the stand mixer with the paddle attachment and a clean bowl; add the cream cheese, peanut butter, brown sugar, and vanilla and beat at high speed until the mixture is smooth and silky.

⑤ Gently fold the cream cheese–peanut butter mixture into the whipped cream with a spatula until completely blended. Spoon into the cooled pie shell and smooth out the top. Place the pie in the freezer for 1 hour or until ready to serve (if you are going to leave it in the freezer awhile, wrap it in plastic wrap after 1 hour so it doesn't get freezer burn).

⑥ Take the pie out of the freezer 15 minutes before serving. Slice it and pig out!

MELTED CHOCOLATE BAR HOT CHOCOLATE
WITH MINT WHIPPED CREAM

Much like mac and cheese, most people think of hot chocolate as a thin, powdery concoction that you get from a box. However, we love showing people that hot chocolate can be a simple, truly stand-out treat when made from scratch. The recipe got its name because every time someone tastes it, they inevitably declare that it tastes just like a melted chocolate bar. To offset the richness of the hot chocolate, we top it off with a dollop of fresh mint whipped cream. Make it once, and you'll never again drink the gross powdered stuff.
Serves 4

MINT WHIPPED CREAM

1/4 cup tightly packed fresh mint leaves

1 tablespoon sugar

1 cup heavy cream

HOT CHOCOLATE

2 cups whole milk

1 cup heavy cream

1/4 cup milk chocolate chips

1 cup semisweet chocolate chips

1 teaspoon pure vanilla extract

2 teaspoons espresso (or espresso powder)

1/8 teaspoon kosher salt

LESSON PLAN

① Make the whipped cream first so that you can put it on the hot chocolate immediately while it's still warm: With a blender or food processor, very briefly pulse the mint leaves, sugar, and cream so that the mint is shredded to tiny pieces, but the cream doesn't get whipped. If you don't have either of these machines, just chop the mint as finely as possible and add it to the cream. With either method, let the mint sit in the cream to infuse it with minty flavor for 5 minutes.

② Strain the cream into a bowl to remove the big pieces of mint. There will still be tiny flecks of mint throughout the cream. Leave them there—they look pretty.

③ With a heavy-duty stand mixer fitted with the whisk attachment at high speed, or by hand with a whisk and a metal bowl, whisk the cream until it forms soft peaks (when you lift the whisk out of the bowl, the beaten cream will form soft peaks that hold their shape).

④ To make the hot chocolate: In a saucepan, heat the milk and cream over medium heat until it is almost boiling, about 5 minutes. Remove from the heat.

⑤ Whisk in the two kinds of chocolate chips, the vanilla, espresso, and salt until the chips are melted and all are thoroughly combined.

⑥ Pour the hot chocolate into 4 small mugs and top each with a dollop of whipped cream. Serve immediately.

DESSERT MAC

When you think of a rich, decadent, sweet dessert, mac and cheese is probably not the first thing that comes to mind.

Thinking that mac and dessert might not go hand-in-hand, we were skeptical ourselves at first. But once we mastered this recipe, we were proved very wrong. Even our staff, who were taste-testers for most of the recipes in this book, said that this was one of their favorite macs. And we believe them, because they were literally licking the plate clean minutes after it came out of the oven. **Serves 6**

1 pound dried wide egg noodles

6 large eggs, lightly beaten

2 teaspoons pure vanilla extract

1/2 cup packed light brown sugar

1/2 cup granulated sugar

2 cups sliced strawberries

1/2 cup raspberry jam

8 ounces mascarpone cheese

2 cups sour cream

1/4 cup unsalted butter, melted

TOPPING

1/2 cup coarsely chopped walnuts

1/2 cup all-purpose flour

1/4 cup packed light brown sugar

3 tablespoons unsalted butter, melted

LESSON PLAN

1. Preheat the oven to 350°F.

2. Cook the egg noodles in salted boiling water until al dente. Drain, and rinse under cold water to stop the cooking process.

3. In a large bowl, mix together the eggs, vanilla, brown sugar, granulated sugar, strawberries, jam, mascarpone, sour cream, and melted butter. Add the pasta and stir to fully combine.

4. In a separate bowl, mix together all of the ingredients for the topping.

5. Spoon the noodle mixture into six 5 by 5-inch oven-proof dishes, and completely cover with a thin layer of topping.

6. Bake until the mixture is bubbly and the topping turns golden brown, about 25 minutes.

7. Serve hot.

BUCKEYES

These cookies resemble the chestnuts that fall from buckeye trees—and are a specialty of Ohio, the "Buckeye State." This is a favorite treat whipped up by a Homeroom neighbor and regular, Carrie Rybczynski. It is an amazing recipe because you can't screw it up—it doesn't even get baked. Feel free to substitute other types of chocolate chips. **Makes 6 dozen**

2 cups crunchy peanut butter

1 cup unsalted butter, at room temperature

1 teaspoon pure vanilla extract

4 cups confectioners' sugar

4 cups semisweet chocolate chips

LESSON PLAN

(1) Line a baking sheet with waxed paper. In a large bowl, mix together the peanut butter, butter, vanilla, and confectioners' sugar. Although the dough may look a little dry, roll it into 1-inch balls and place them on the prepared baking sheet. (Depending on how closely you space the dough balls, you may need 2 baking sheets.)

(2) Press a toothpick into the top of each ball to be used later as a handle for dipping, and place the filled baking sheet(s) in the freezer until firm, about 30 minutes.

(3) Melt the chocolate chips in the microwave or in a double boiler, stirring frequently until smooth. Some people own double boilers, but you can also make one by setting a metal bowl holding the chips over a pan of hot water simmering on the stove—the indirect heat makes the chips melt perfectly. Just be sure that none of the steaming water gets into the chocolate chip bowl because the water causes chocolate to get chunky and not melt properly.

(4) Holding on to the toothpicks, dip each frozen peanut butter ball into the chocolate. Leave a small portion of the tops of the balls undipped so they look like buckeyes! Refrigerate the cookies until the chocolate firms up, about an hour, and keep them chilled until serving.

STRAWBERRY CRISP

This dessert is a great summery treat because you don't have to bake the entire dish—only the topping goes in the oven for about ten minutes, so it'll keep your house nice and cool on a hot day. Plus, you get to enjoy the freshness of the berries at their peak. With a layer of fresh macerated berries (berries that have been mixed with sugar to bring out their juices), crunchy crisp, and a dollop of fresh whipped cream—you can't go wrong. You can also try it with other summer fruit—though you will want to adjust the amount of sugar depending on the sweetness of the fruit, and probably omit the balsamic vinegar. **Serves 4**

1 pound strawberries, stemmed and quartered

3 tablespoons granulated sugar

1 tablespoon balsamic vinegar

1 cup unsalted butter, melted

1 3/4 cups all-purpose flour

1/2 cup graham cracker crumbs

1/4 cup packed light brown sugar

Whipped cream (see Mint Whipped Cream, page 98, or you can use store-bought)

LESSON PLAN

1. Preheat the oven to 400°F. In a bowl, mix the strawberries, granulated sugar, and balsamic vinegar. Let stand for at least 20 minutes.

2. In a mixing bowl, stir together the butter, flour, graham cracker crumbs, and brown sugar. Spread on a baking sheet, and pat down the mixture on the sheet with a spatula.

3. Bake the crumb mixture until it turns light brown, about 10 minutes. Let cool completely on the baking sheet, then break it up into little chunks using the spatula.

4. To serve, spoon the macerated strawberries with some of the liquid into individual bowls, top with crumbly topping, and a healthy dose of whipped cream.

LIME BARS

Although many people know and love lemon bars, we think that substituting the tart complexity of limes for lemons makes this buttery dessert even better. For those of you who are afraid of making pie crusts, this recipe is an awesome, nonscary place to start. You don't have to roll it out, refrigerate it, or even shape it. You just mix up the ingredients and press it into the bottom of a pan. For the filling, you just whisk it together, pour it in, and bake it up. Simple, mouth-puckering deliciousness. **Makes 8 bars**

LIME CRUST

1 cup all-purpose flour

1/4 cup confectioners' sugar

1 tablespoon finely grated lime zest

1/2 cup unsalted butter, chilled and cut into small pieces

Pinch of kosher salt

LIME FILLING

1 1/2 cups confectioners' sugar

2 tablespoons all-purpose flour

1/2 teaspoon baking powder

3 large eggs

1/2 cup freshly squeezed lime juice

LESSON PLAN

1. Preheat the oven to 350°F. Butter an 8-inch square baking pan.

2. For the crust: Place the flour, confectioners' sugar, zest, butter, and salt in a food processor (preferably) or use an electric mixer. Pulse until the mixture resembles sand. Firmly and evenly press the mixture into the bottom of the prepared baking pan, and bake until golden brown, about 30 minutes. Leave the oven on.

3. Meanwhile, make the filling: In a bowl, whisk together the confectioners' sugar, flour, and baking powder. In another bowl, beat the eggs on high speed with an electric mixer until they have doubled in volume, 1 to 2 minutes. Decrease the speed of the mixer to low and add the sugar mixture and lime juice and mix until blended.

4. Pour the filling into the hot crust and bake until the filling in the center is set (does not jiggle), about 15 minutes.

5. Let cool in the pan before cutting and serving.

GRASSHOPPER PIE
WITH HOMEMADE CHOCOLATE SAUCE

If you were to come in to Homeroom on a warm sunny day in the summer, you'd see at least five people with green ice cream running down their chins, as they happily scoop crushed-up chocolate cookies, mint ice cream, and chocolate sauce out of mason jars. (We are huge fans of things in jars—from local beers to our homemade desserts.)

This is an easy dessert to make in a pinch. It's rich and delicious, plus the homemade sauce only takes a few minutes and turns this treat from great to ridiculously addictive. **Serves 4**

HOMEMADE CHOCOLATE SAUCE

1 cup water

1/2 cup sugar

1/2 cup light corn syrup

3/4 cup cocoa powder

1/2 cup semisweet chocolate chips

1/2 cup heavy cream

GRASSHOPPER PIE

1 pint mint chocolate chip ice cream

8 to 10 chocolate wafer cookies, crumbled

LESSON PLAN

1. To make the chocolate sauce: In a small saucepan over low heat, whisk together the water, sugar, light corn syrup, and cocoa powder.

2. When the mixture begins to simmer, remove the pan from the heat and add the chocolate chips and cream. Continue whisking until the sauce is smooth. Let cool completely before pouring it over the ice cream. Store any extra sauce in an airtight container in the refrigerator for up to 3 days.

3. To assemble: Put a small scoop of ice cream in each of four 8-ounce mason jars.

4. Follow with a layer of cookies and a drizzle of chocolate sauce.

5. Repeat the layers until you get to the top of the jar. The last layer should be chocolate sauce.

HOMEMADE OREOS

Our customers are obsessed with these cookies—we sell twice as many of them as we do any other dessert, and they've won awards in the area. The filling is remarkably similar to the stuff you grew up on, but the cookie is a million times better. Soft, chocolaty, and with a little salt sprinkled on top to contrast with the sweet filling, it is the most addictive treat we've ever eaten. This recipe is adapted from a version we found on the awesome blog *Smitten Kitchen*. **Makes 15 cookies**

CHOCOLATE COOKIES

1¼ cups all-purpose flour

½ cup cocoa powder

1½ cups granulated sugar

1 teaspoon baking soda

¼ teaspoon baking powder

¼ teaspoon table salt

½ cup plus 2 tablespoons unsalted butter, at room temperature

2 large eggs

2 teaspoons kosher salt or flaky sea salt, for topping

VANILLA FILLING

¼ cup unsalted butter, at room temperature

¼ cup vegetable shortening

2 cups sifted confectioners' sugar

2 teaspoons pure vanilla extract

LESSON PLAN

1. Preheat the oven to 375°F. Line a baking sheet with parchment paper.

2. To make the cookies: In a heavy-duty stand mixer fitted with the paddle attachment or in a food processor, mix the flour, cocoa powder, sugar, baking soda, baking powder, and salt on low speed. Still on low, add the ½ cup plus 2 tablespoons butter and the eggs, and blend until the mixture resembles sand.

3. Scoop out tablespoon-size balls of dough and arrange 2 inches apart on the prepared baking sheet (they'll spread as they bake). Sprinkle the topping salt over all the cookies. Bake until the dough just begins to crack and puff up a little, about 6 minutes. Let the cookies cool on the sheet. They will look underdone when you take them out—but they will harden more as they cool and achieve a perfect softness. If you take them out when they have fully baked, they will be hard, crunchy, and nowhere near as delicious.

CONTINUED

④ To make the filling: Using a heavy-duty stand mixer fitted with the paddle attachment, blend the butter and the shortening, while slowly adding in the confectioners' sugar and vanilla, until smooth.

⑤ Using a pastry bag, or a heavy-duty plastic bag with a tip cut off one corner, pipe a layer of filling around the edges of half of the cookies, and a dot in the center. Take the remaining cookies and press them on top of the filling. Enjoy! These cookies can be stored for up to two days in an airtight container.

BEST-EVER BROWNIES

Seriously

Everyone likes to claim that their brownie is the best, but in our case, we're pretty sure it's true. We experimented with tons of variations before settling on this recipe. A fudgy brownie dotted with chocolate chips for intense chocolaty bursts—it is a decadent treat best enjoyed with a big, cold glass of milk. We've had this dessert on our menu since opening day and it has its own fan base of people who come in for brownies alone. As far as chocolate chips go, the darker the chocolate, the more intense the chocolaty taste— we recommend Ghirardelli's 60% Cacao Bittersweet Chocolate Baking Chips.

The biggest trick to getting soft, moist brownies is to not overmix the batter in step 4. The most common rookie baking mistake we see is that people like to mix the batter until it is smooth. Doing so will unfortunately make the finished product hard as a brick—and this is true of all baked goods other than bread. So it's a good habit to break if you are a chronic overmixer. Leave a few lumps in there—stop mixing when you don't see white streaks of flour anymore and you'll be good to go. **Makes 12 hefty brownies, or 20 smaller ones**

1 (12-ounce) bag (about 2 cups) chocolate chips

1 cup unsalted butter

1 1/2 cups granulated sugar

1/2 cup packed light brown sugar

5 large eggs, lightly beaten

2 teaspoons pure vanilla extract

2 1/2 cups all-purpose flour

1 teaspoon table salt

2 tablespoons cocoa powder

LESSON PLAN

1. Preheat the oven to 350°F. Butter an 11 by 7-inch baking pan.

2. Set aside 1/2 cup of the chocolate chips for later. Melt the rest of the chips along with the butter in a double boiler set over medium heat. If you don't have a double boiler (or don't know what the heck that is), microwave the butter and chocolate chips for 20 seconds at a time, stirring in between, until they have both melted completely and can be stirred together.

3. Off of the heat, whisk the granulated sugar, brown sugar, eggs, and vanilla into the liquid chocolate-butter mixture.

CONTINUED

④ In a separate bowl, whisk together the flour, salt, and cocoa powder. Gently fold the flour mixture into the chocolate-egg mixture, along with the reserved 1/2 cup of chocolate chips. Do NOT overmix (see headnote)!

⑤ Pour the batter into the prepared baking dish, and bake for 40 minutes. Remove from the oven and let cool before cutting. (NOTE: Most brownie recipes will tell you to test for doneness by sticking a toothpick into the brownies, and if it comes out clean, the brownies are done. We don't recommend this method for this recipe—the batter should still be underbaked in the middle. But as the brownies cool, the center part will continue cooking until it is moist and fudgy. If you take the brownies out when the toothpick is clean, they will keep cooking and overbake.)

ABOUT THE AUTHORS

Dan Jung

ALLISON AREVALO started cooking pretty much when she was able to stand. Born into a food-loving Italian family in New York, she helped her great-grandmother cook massive meals for Sunday family dinners and learned the basics of cooking in that kitchen. Allison pursued a career as a marketing exec in NYC before deciding to follow her true passion in life: food. In 2008, Allison and her husband took a leap of faith: they quit their jobs and drove across the country to Oakland, CA, in hopes of one day opening a restaurant. Allison freelanced as a food writer and created the *Local Lemons* food blog, which showcased her original recipes. It received high accolades from Saveur.com, CNN, Serious Eats, and WSJ.com, among others. Her dream came true in 2011, the year she and Erin opened the doors to Homeroom.

ERIN WADE is a chef-turned-attorney-turned-chef-again. Erin's love for cooking was sparked by her father's homemade mac and cheese and her mother's vast cookbook collection. While receiving her undergraduate degree at Princeton, Erin was a restaurant critic for the *Daily Princetonian* and apprenticed at night in the kitchen of a local French restaurant. Upon graduating, Erin worked as a line cook and in pastry at restaurants in New York before attending law school at Berkeley. After practicing law for a year, Erin came to her senses and decided to return to her love of cooking by opening Homeroom with Allison. She lives in Oakland with her husband, Uri, and her daughter, Ellie—her favorite cooking partners.

MEASUREMENT CONVERSION CHARTS

	U.S.	Imperial	Metric
Volume	1 tablespoon	1/2 fl oz	15 ml
	2 tablespoons	1 fl oz	30 ml
	1/4 cup	2 fl oz	60 ml
	1/3 cup	3 fl oz	90 ml
	1/2 cup	4 fl oz	120 ml
	2/3 cup	5 fl oz (1/4 pint)	150 ml
	3/4 cup	6 fl oz	180 ml
	1 cup	8 fl oz (1/3 pint)	240 ml
	11/4 cups	10 fl oz (1/2 pint)	300 ml
	2 cups (1 pint)	16 fl oz (2/3 pint)	480 ml
	21/2 cups	20 fl oz (1 pint)	600 ml
	1 quart	32 fl oz (12/3 pints)	1 L

	Fahrenheit	Celsius/Gas Mark
Temperature	250°F	120°C/gas mark 1/2
	275°F	135°C/gas mark 1
	300°F	150°C/gas mark 2
	325°F	160°C/gas mark 3
	350°F	180 or 175°C/gas mark 4
	375°F	190°C/gas mark 5
	400°F	200°C/gas mark 6
	425°F	220°C/gas mark 7
	450°F	230°C/gas mark 8
	475°F	245°C/gas mark 9
	500°F	260°C

	Inch	Metric
Length	1/4 inch	6 mm
	1/2 inch	1.25 cm
	3/4 inch	2 cm
	1 inch	2.5 cm
	6 inches (1/2 foot)	15 cm
	12 inches (1 foot)	30 cm

	U.S./Imperial	Metric
Weight	1/2 oz	15 g
	1 oz	30 g
	2 oz	60 g
	1/4 lb	115 g
	1/3 lb	150 g
	1/2 lb	225 g
	3/4 lb	350 g
	1 lb	450 g

INDEX

Published in the United States by Ten Speed Press, an imprint of the
Crown Publishing Group, a division of Random House, Inc., New York
www.crownpublishing.com
www.tenspeed.com

Ten Speed Press and the Ten Speed Press colophon are registered
trademarks of Random House, Inc.

Library of Congress Cataloging-in-Publication Data
Arevalo, Allison, 1979–
  The mac + cheese cookbook : 50 simple recipes from homeroom,
America's favorite mac and cheese restaurant / Allison Arevalo and
Erin Wade ; photography by Sara Remington.
      pages cm
1. Cooking (Pasta) 2. Cooking (Cheese) 3. Casserole cooking.
I. Wade, Erin, 1981– II. Title.
  TX809.M17A74 2013
  641.82'2—dc23
                              2013001194

Hardcover ISBN: 978-1-60774-466-5
eBook ISBN: 978-1-60774-467-2

Printed in China

Design and illustrations by Betsy Stromberg
Food and prop styling by Christine Wolheim

10 9

First Edition